P9-AQL-983

# FEAST

## BY FIRELIGHT

To Mamma and Papa,
for bringing me into this world with
unconditional love and support

To Bobby and Ayla,
my two greatest loves

# FEAST
## BY FIRELIGHT

**SIMPLE RECIPES**
for camping, cabins, and
the great outdoors

Emma Frisch

Photography by
Christina Holmes

TEN SPEED PRESS
California | New York

# contents

# introduction

*The only real effort required to have*
*a feast by firelight is to get outside, spark a fire,*
*and roast something simple, like a sausage.*
*Mother Nature provides the rest:*
*moonlight, woodsmoke, moss cushions,*
*and a forest symphony.*

Before the advent of sturdy homes and urban living, most meals were an outdoor affair in a world of digital-free connection. And while these types of meals are no longer a daily ritual, there is still something magical and eternal about eating under the open sky. It is something our ancestors have done in community throughout time to celebrate the earth's abundance. This book will show you how easy it is to create a modern-day feast by firelight.

In 2014, my husband, Bobby, and I opened Firelight Camps, our "glamping" destination in Ithaca, New York. We were so focused on the quality of our guests' experiences that our own meals often took a back seat. One night after a long day, I squeezed in around the campfire and lay an iron grate over the coals. I pulled lightly seasoned skirt steak from a ziplock bag and placed it on the grill, surrounding it with summer vegetables. I shifted the food with tongs until the meat caramelized and the peppers blistered. I then transferred the steak to a wooden cutting board, sliced it, and spooned pungent salsa verde over the top. Just then, Bobby joined me. We clinked our forks and tucked in to our simple meal.

I looked up from my plate because the crowd had gone silent. "What are you eating?" asked a young man. "It smells amazing." Maybe he wasn't looking for handouts but I felt compelled by his question to share our meal with the others gathered around the flames. I sliced our food into bite-size pieces and passed them around, listing the ingredients in my mamma's salsa verde. This is how *Feast by Firelight* was born, and what this book is all about: quick outdoor meals meant to be shared with family and friends, old and new.

If you're drawn to this book, you're probably a lot like me. I love to cook, I love to eat, and I love to be outside. I didn't go to culinary school, but I was trained by someone just as good, my Italian mother, who often started our lessons in the garden.

When I was growing up, my mother believed fresh food and fresh air were key to raising healthy children—all four of them! I was only two years old when I had my first foraging adventure with my twin sister, Dimity. Wearing our undies and red Wellington boots, we set off into our backyard vegetable patch to pluck tomatoes from the vines. When we outgrew the backyard, weekends and family holidays were spent exploring state parks, and, inevitably, Mamma brought a picnic basket.

My mother was the Houdini of alfresco meals, putting out a whole spread in seconds, complete with cloth napkins and metal forks. Sometimes, to our complete embarrassment, she would

Me and my siblings with friends at the top of a trail in the Dolomites in northeastern Italy.

My mother preparing our new vegetable garden with her little helpers, me and my twin sister.

pull off the road, whip out the pruning shears she kept in the glove box, and cut honeysuckle stems or other wild flowers to dress up the picnic table. My three siblings and I would duck down in our seats, praying our friends wouldn't drive by and see our mother's wild hair tangled with the blossoms. Eating together was the cornerstone of our childhood and not to be missed, even on the trail.

It wasn't until I trained as a backcountry guide in college that I realized my family was unique. My group was trekking through the Dolly Sods Wilderness of West Virginia when, absentmindedly, I dunked my hand into a bag of gorp (good ol' raisins and peanuts) that the leader had doled out. Ouch! I nearly cracked a tooth on a Jolly Rancher! I'm not a purist but I have a hard time swallowing the fact that processed food, prepackaged shortcuts, and expensive dehydrated meal packets have come to define camping food. Not only is this at odds with my upbringing but with the very notion of getting back to nature—the source of who we are and what we eat.

So during training, I took over meal planning for our group, packing snacks like dried fruit, cured salami, and blocks of aged cheddar. Over the next decade, I blazed my own trail as I stepped into the roles of trip leader, rock climber, and mountaineer, and built my career in camp cuisine as a chef and food blogger. Finally, I brought my love for food and the outdoors together under one tent at Firelight Camps.

*Feast by Firelight* will take you back to the roots of camp cooking, though I don't expect you to hunt for your own dinner. In this dependable guide to cooking outdoors, you'll find a collection of stories, simple recipes, and tips that I've refined over countless outdoor adventures. It is my hope that this book will inspire your own cookouts, inviting you to fall more deeply in sync with the people around you, yourself, and the great outdoors.

# how to use this book

I go into the wild to still the noise inside my mind. I feel as if I've come alive when pockets of evergreen perfume drift inside my nose and the soft murmur of creeks trickle into my ears. Being outdoors heightens the senses in every way, cultivating an ideal mind-set for cooking.

Humans have always relied on sensory cues for making meals, and written recipes are no exception. Dishes need to be understood not just with taste but also with sight, scent, sound, and touch. When I competed on *Food Network Star*, I showed an audience of four hundred people how to massage cabbage for a slaw. Wiggling my fingers in the air, I said, "Don't forget your most important tool!" The judges loved it, because they knew it was true.

Cooking outdoors is an opportunity to fine-tune our senses, a practice easily lost when we judge grilled chicken from an image in a book or on a screen. A Dutch oven and timer are helpful but it's the smell of toasted, sweet kernels that slaps me in the face, telling me the cornbread is ready. We're built with tools as equally important as pots and pans, and there's hardly a better time to use these gifts than when we're in nature.

To start you off, I'll give you all the nuts and bolts for creating your essential outdoor kitchen, whether you're a minimalist or a car camper. I'll also talk you through other fundamentals such as packing your cooler and starting a fire. Then we'll dive into the recipes, which I've made as simple and camp-friendly as possible. Also, I've indicated whether they are gluten-free and/or vegetarian with these GF V icons. And finally, I've provided menu ideas for all kinds of camping trips, from a simple family car-camping weekend to a rough-and-ready, off-the-grid experience.

I follow general rules of thumb when cooking, and I've listed them on the following pages to guide you in using this book. With these tips, you'll get the best results every time—no matter where you are.

# tips for outdoor cooking

**Use your senses** Rarely do two people interpret a recipe the same way. There will also be variables like wind, a warped pan, or a different brand of an ingredient that can affect the outcome. Luckily, you have your senses to help guide you. Implement them, and listen to your intuition.

**Prep** Many of my recipes have a "Prep" section. This alerts you to what is best prepared at home so that cooking your meal will be quick, easy, and fun once you arrive at camp (with fewer dishes to wash!). Of course, you can also prepare nearly everything outside without doing anything in advance. The main method describes how to finish the recipe at your campsite using your prepped ingredients.

**Pack food in reusable containers and bags**
Ziplock bags are portable, space saving, and leak proof. Even so, I'm still wary of mixing plastic and food and am conscious of plastic's environmental impact. If you can, use alternatives, such as silicone food-storage bags, Bee's Wrap (a beeswax-coated fabric that works like plastic wrap), and stainless-steel or glass containers. Otherwise, wash, hang dry, and reuse your ziplock bags.

**Keep your food "chilled"**
Depending on where you are, use your home refrigerator or camp cooler to keep your food chilled. My food storage recommendations are always based on the assumption that you are using the freshest ingredients possible. In some recipes, you will see recommendations for storing food at "ambient" temperature, which will vary based on where you're camping. Also see "How to Pack Your Cooler" on page 16.

**Shop at farm stands** A great way to find fresh produce is at roadside stands or farmers' markets en route to your campsite. It will be more nutritious from having just been harvested, giving you an extra boost when you're exerting yourself outside! Small-scale farmers and gardeners are often organic and non-GMO but don't carry certifications or labels. Ask if they are; you'll feel better about buying food that minimizes harm to the environment and our bodies.

**Use local honey** This golden liquid gives you a taste of the region's flora, and is easy to track down at roadside stands and nearby markets. My nonna swore that honey was the cure-all for scrapes, burns, or bruises, and it can also help stave off localized pollen allergies while boosting your immune system. No one wants to get sick on a camping trip. Properly seal and stow your honey before going to bed, especially in bear territory.

**Choosing salt** Kosher salt is versatile, effective, and my go-to for cooking and seasoning. For baking, I prefer fine salt, which measures more consistently and is evenly distributed in your final dish. For garnishing, I like to use coarse sea salt—large crystals or flakes—which adds a mineral flavor and delightful crunch. My favorite is *sel gris*, or gray sea salt.

We have a responsibility to take care of Mother Earth and help preserve the wild places in which we like to play. With this in mind, the Leave No Trace Center for Outdoor Ethics (LNT.org) created the Leave No Trace Seven Principles as a quick guide for treading lightly outside.

1 Plan Ahead and Prepare

2 Travel and Camp on Durable Surfaces

3 Dispose of Waste Properly

4 Leave What You Find

5 Minimize Campfire Impacts

6 Respect Wildlife

7 Be Considerate of Other Visitors

leave no trace

**Use freshly ground black pepper** I always call for freshly ground black pepper because it's so much more flavorful. Small, portable pepper mills are available in the spice section of your grocery store. In my recipes, I specify the amount of pepper used by turns of the pepper mill: ten turns is ¼ teaspoon, and twenty turns is ½ teaspoon.

**Use fresh baking soda and baking powder** Make sure these ingredients are fresh or you'll end up with a bitter, metallic taste in your food. Choose aluminum-free baking powder, such as Rumford, to help eliminate any chance of a "tinny" taste. Expired baking soda can be kept on hand for squelching grease fires (see page 26).

**Get a microplane—your camp kit's best friend** Also known as a fine grater or zester, this space-saving, lightweight tool is the best way to grate your garlic and ginger and to zest lemons.

**Adjust the heat on your camp stove** Camp stoves have a limited range of heat and may burn hotter as a result of being fueled by propane. You may need to adjust the recipes in this book based on your camp stove; for example, if I suggest medium heat, you may need to adjust your knob to medium-low, or even low. Use the height and volume of the flames as your guide.

**Factor in charcoal time** For recipes on the grill, factor in 15 minutes to light your charcoal and fire up the grill.

**Grease the grill** After firing up the grill, clean the grill grate before cooking; residue comes off more easily when the grate is hot. Use the back of a metal spatula to scrape the grill clean, giving it a final polish with a wire grill brush. Then, grease the grate. You can use a grill mop (literally, a tiny mop!) or use tongs to rub a wad of paper towel with vegetable oil over the hot grate. Even if your food is well coated with oil, greasing will prevent any chance of sticking. Do this before and after cooking, so you pay it forward to the next camping party.

**Dispose of cooking and dish-water** Use a camping-style pot with a "strainer lid," or create a toothpick-size crack between the lid and pot, and hold both firmly with your hands while tilting the pot and draining the water away from you. In both cases, pour the water through a fine-mesh tea strainer (or pantyhose!) into another vessel. Scatter the water in various places beyond your campsite so that it's not concentrated in one spot. This minimizes the chance of attracting wildlife to your campsite and habituating them to human food.

**Prepare for first aid** No one plans for an accident. Be smart and prepared, and bring a first aid kit.

# the essential outdoor kitchen

When Annie Farrell took me under her wing at Millstone Farm in Connecticut, she taught me something that was more important than how to grow vegetables: *"Use it up, wear it out, make it do, or do without."* I learned the value of repurposing common objects that I had been throwing away. She turned an old clothes dryer into a salad spinner, empty water jugs into tiny greenhouses, and ratty T-shirts into sweatbands. This philosophy stuck with me. There are so many shiny new things to buy for camping, but if there's one place you don't need something shiny and new, it's the great outdoors. So patch your tents, clean your grandma's cast-iron pan, and be resourceful with food storage.

My outdoor kitchen is tried, true, and minimalist and perfectly equipped to prepare any recipe in this book. If you want to pare down your kitchen even more, cross-check this list with the tools and equipment called for in your chosen recipes. If a recipe requires a special tool that is not included here, I will mention it in the recipe.

# how to pack your outdoor kitchen

With the exception of the large items under "Stove, Grill, and Open Fire," all of your gear will fit in one 54-quart plastic tub. If you choose space-efficient nesting pots and pans with pot lifters, you'll have even more wiggle room. It's nice to have a picnic table or portable camp table for laying out your gear once you arrive at camp; your tub can then be repurposed as an on-site sink or for storing dirty dishware. Wrap greasy or dirty items, like cast-iron pans or a grill brush, in newspaper before packing them in the storage tub. The optional items depend on the recipes you choose. Bring a shovel if you're planning to dig your own campfire pit or cook with coals.

**Tip:** Wrap sharp tools in a dish towel and secure with rubber bands. Wrap again in your apron.

## TOOLS AND SERVINGWARE

- Multipurpose pocket knife with corkscrew, bottle opener, and scissors

- Chef's knife, sharpened

- Paring knife, sharpened

- Cutting board (bring two if preparing meat *and* veggies; silicone boards are lightweight and packable, while wood are nice for serving)

- 12 by 17-inch rimmed baking sheet

- Serving spoon

- Wooden spoon or stainless-steel slotted spoon

- Long-handled metal grill tongs (bring two if grilling meat *and* veggies)

- Long-handled metal grill spatula (extra-long for grilling)

- Microplane (fine zester or grater)

- Meat thermometer

- 3-inch fine-mesh strainer

- Apron

- Coffee gear

- Individual camper place settings

- Large mixing bowl (optional)

- Large or small serving bowls and plates (optional)

- Small whisk (optional)

- Pastry brush (optional)

- Vegetable peeler (optional)

- Serrated bread knife (optional)

- Paper towels (optional)

- Tablecloth or picnic blanket (optional)

- Birthday candles (for whoever's has just passed or is approaching)

## POTS AND PANS

- 10-inch cast-iron skillet, frying pan, or sauté pan, with lid

- 12-inch cast-iron skillet, frying pan or sauté pan, with lid

- 1-quart pot

- 3-quart pot

- 5-quart cast-iron Dutch oven, with flanged-lid

- Dutch oven lid-lifter (optional)

    *Bring just the pots and pans needed for your recipes and choose sizes that nest for efficient packing. Various camping brands make lightweight, space-saving cookware with potholders. These often come with "strainer" lids so you can leave the colander at home (or see "Dispose of cooking and dishwater" on page 9). If baking with a Dutch oven over coals, a flanged lid is ideal. For less cleanup, serve directly from pots and pans.*

## STORAGE AND CLEANING SUPPLIES

- Glass jar with lid for collecting grease and cooking fat

- Extra containers and large ziplock bags for leftovers

- 1 box heavy-duty aluminum foil

- 1 box parchment or butcher paper (for serving certain dishes; less bulk and washing)

- 2 to 4 quick-dry dish towels or bandannas (make sure you don't mind stains, and designate one for using with cast iron)

- Biodegradable, eco-friendly soap

- 3 trash bags per day for trash, recycling, and compost (seal and store properly at night to keep critters away)

- Silicone sponge (dries quickly)

- Water, if not available on-site (water "bladders" or bags are great collapsible options)

## STOVE, GRILL, AND OPEN FIRE

- Matches or a lighter

- Two-burner camp stove

- Propane for camp stove (see page 24)

- Portable grill and/or grill grate

- Wire grill brush

- Charcoal

- Charcoal chimney

- Welding gloves

- Newspaper

- Shovel

**Tip:** Save on washing by licking your plate or mopping it clean with bread. Scrape off remaining residue with coarse salt or good old-fashioned dirt, a natural abrasive sponge! Plus, a little bit of dirt is good for you.

# how to pack your cooler

Camping can hold enough uncertainties that you don't want to add food poisoning to the mix. The illustration on the facing page shows you how to properly pack and store your food, with additional recommendations in the recipes. I suggest making time for all food prep the night before your trip, to ensure you'll have the freshest food once at camp. For food storage beyond 24 hours, my favorite resource to consult is www.stilltasty.com, which offers food storage times for individual ingredients, in every form (e.g., raw, cooked, chopped, whole, etc.). Here are a few extra tips for packing more common ingredients called for throughout the book.

- Never pack warm food!

- Unless using for other recipes, portion liquids (such as milk or oil) into smaller containers.

- Seal shredded cheese in a ziplock bag or airtight container and then chill for up to 5 days.

- Make sure bacon is sealed tightly in its packaging; if wrapped in butcher paper, transfer to a ziplock bag and then chill for up to 5 days.

- Rinse herbs and shake off excess water. Pack them whole (leaves attached to stems) in a moist paper towel, seal in a ziplock bag, and then chill for up to 3 days. Basil is the exception, which is best planted in a jar of water (like a flower bouquet) and balanced in a cup holder en route to camp. Otherwise, wrap in a moist paper towel in a ziplock bag, as described, for up to 24 hours at ambient temperature; do *not* chill or the leaves will blacken.

- Pack eggs (raw or hard-boiled) in an egg carton. To save space, cut the carton to hold the total number of eggs you plan to bring (for all recipes).

- Pack dry ingredients and pantry items (including onions, potatoes, and garlic) in reusable shopping bags.

### COOLER

- Choose a thick-walled cooler for better insulation.

- Wheels are handy.

- Scrub the cooler sparkling clean before packing.

- Store the cooler in a shady spot.

- Minimize opening the cooler.

- Pack drinks in a separate cooler—you'll be opening it more!

### ICE

- Make large chunks of ice by freezing water in ziplock bags or containers. They will melt slower and can be crushed into smaller pieces for drinks.

- Hold ice in ziplock bags to help keep things dry as it melts.

- Layer ice in between food.

- Drain melted ice-water regularly.

### PACKING

- Pack food in leakproof containers or ziplock bags.

- Pack frozen items straight from the freezer, to double as ice packs and last longer.

- Pack heavier, sturdier foods on bottom.

- Use a thin cutting board or baking sheet to separate meat, poultry, and seafood from fruits and vegetables.

- Place a towel on top for extra insulation and to prevent hot air pockets.

# how to pack your pantry

The recipes in this book pack plenty of flavor, but it's always nice to have basic staples and extra seasoning on hand. Your storage methods will help ensure a lightweight, user-friendly pantry. Here are some tips.

- Pack any containers that might spill into a ziplock bag, even if you think they are sealed tightly. Chances are they will still leak, and you don't want to end up like my little brother, Sebastian, whose duffel bag smells like fish sauce forevermore.

- Pack dry seasoning in 4-ounce jars, small containers, or small ziplock bags.

- Pack extra spices in a "stacking bead kit" from your local craft store (small containers with lids that screw on top of one another). These are excellent traveling spice kits; load them up with four to six of your favorite spices.

- Pack ground coffee in a ziplock bag.

- Transfer smaller amounts of honey, oil, and vinegar from your home stock into small, portable jars or squeeze bottles based on the amount you'll need for each recipe. If bringing the whole bottle, bring liquor pourers so you can replace the cap for easy drizzling. You can also purchase individual packets of honey, oil, and other condiments such as nut butter.

## BASICS

- Baking soda (for putting out grease fires)

- Box of unsalted butter (in addition to the amount called for in your recipes)

- Condiments (e.g., ketchup, mustard, mayo; see pages 30 to 32)

- Hot sauce or red pepper flakes

- Cooking oil, such as coconut or sunflower oil

- Olive oil

- Salt; kosher or fine salt for cooking and coarse sea salt for garnishing

- Small peppercorn mill (find in the spice section at your grocery store)

- Sweetener (e.g., honey, maple syrup, your preferred sugar, or other sweetener)

- Vinegar (my favorites are apple cider or red wine)

- Zesty Za'atar (see page 33)

# bring the heat

campfires
camp stoves
grills

When cooking outdoors, there are a variety of heat sources to choose from. This section will introduce you to the three most common you can find, bring, or create at your camping area, and the necessary tools for each.

# building a campfire

The campfire is an ancient, time-honored circle—a ceremony—around which people connect with themselves, each other, and the natural world. Even today, a camping trip isn't complete until we've saturated our hair and clothes with the smell of wood smoke, drawn warmth and light into our souls, and watched our worries be swept up and away like sparks into the night sky. Use these guidelines and safety tips to maximize your campfire experience.

- Clear 10 feet of tall, hanging, or loose debris that could catch fire, such as branches, grass, leaves, and your gear!

- Dig a hole about 1 foot deep and 3 feet wide—you'll need a shovel.

- Make a circle border of large, dry rocks around the pit.

- Loosely pile about four wads of newspaper (tinder) in the center of the fire pit. Keep extra newspaper on hand.

- Collect sticks and twigs (kindling) about the thickness of your thumb and arrange them like a tepee, resting lightly on the newspaper.

- Light the tinder and blow gently to help the kindling catch. (Safely discard used matches to prevent forest fires.)

- Once the kindling catches fire, carefully arrange four large, dry logs (see "Firewood 101," page 23) over the kindling, meeting in the middle to form a tepee. Leave a few inches of space between the kindling and logs for air flow.

## PUTTING OUT YOUR CAMPFIRE

1. Allow the wood to burn completely to ash, if possible.

2. Pour lots of water on the fire until the hissing sound stops.

3. If you don't have water, bury the fire and embers with dirt or sand. Use a shovel to scrape embers from sticks and logs to make sure there are no exposed or smoldering embers left behind.

4. Embers too hot to touch are too hot to leave. Continue adding water, dirt, or sand and stirring with a shovel until all the material is cool.

## PICKING A LOCATION

1. Don't build a campfire if it is prohibited on the property.

2. Don't build a campfire in dry or drought conditions; a forest fire is far worse than cold feet—or cold dinner.

3. Find out if the area has existing fire rings or pits you can use to minimize impact to the land.

4. If you're creating a fire pit, choose an open site free of low-hanging branches, plant life, and other flammable objects. Be sure the fire pit is at least 20 feet from any tent.

5. Choose a spot that's protected from strong gusts of wind.

## MAINTAINING YOUR CAMPFIRE

1. Stack logs upwind from the fire so you don't risk them catching on fire from stray sparks. Add them to the fire as needed.

2. Keep your fire at a manageable size. Have a source of water, a bucket, and a shovel nearby at all times in case the fire gets out of control.

3. Don't burn items that can explode, shatter, and/or create harmful fumes or dust, such as aerosol cans, pressurized containers, glass, or aluminum cans.

4. Never leave your campfire unattended, and make certain children and pets are supervised near the fire.

# firewood 101

Collecting firewood is fun and feels primal but it isn't as simple as foraging for fallen branches. Wood (even rotting or kiln-dried wood) is teeming with life, from insects and larvae to fungus spores; we want those species to remain in their native habitat. When we move firewood more than 50 miles from where it was harvested, we risk transferring invasive species to other forests, and depleting those forests for generations to come. But it's not so glum. Follow these simple protocols and you'll be sourcing firewood with the forest's best interests in mind!

- **Do not use treated wood.** Scrap wood from construction sites, abandoned fences, and other structural ruins may have been treated with chemicals for durability or contain paint residue, which are highly toxic when burned.

- **When purchasing bundled or cord firewood,** ask the seller if it was harvested within 50 miles.

- **If you must buy firewood farther than 50 miles from your campsite,** look for a United States Department of Agriculture, or USDA, APHIS seal that certifies it was heat-treated to kill pests.

- **When foraging for firewood near your campsite,** look for dry wood that is brown or gray ("green" materials won't burn), sounds hollow when tapped, is lightweight, or has cracked ends or peeling bark.

## testing the heat

| SECONDS | HEAT |
| --- | --- |
| 2 to 3 | high |
| 4 | medium-high |
| 5 to 6 | medium |
| 7 to 8 | medium-low |
| 9 to 12 | low |

For me, cooking is rooted in intuition and observation. But it's also helpful to understand the temperature of the fire. Here's a way to test the heat: Wait until the flames and smoke have subsided and a fine gray ash covers the coals. Then, hold your hand 4 to 5 inches above the coals. Using full counts (one-potato, two-potato, three-potato . . .), see how long, in seconds, you can keep your hand there.

Remember that factors such as wind and air temperature can affect heat level and cooking times. With practice, you'll build confidence and be able to know when your food is cooked. Part of the fun of cooking outdoors is that no two fires are the same; over time, you'll gain experience and insights that will help you understand heat well beyond this hand count. Still, this is a wonderful baseline that even professionals like myself turn to for guidance.

# fueling a camp stove

The recipes in this book are designed for cooking on a camp stove or campground grill. While I recommend using hardwood lump charcoal for the grill, you'll need propane, white gas, or a blend to power your camp stove.

Propane is a liquefied gas that burns blue and is used as fuel for engines, central heating, and, of course, grills and portable stoves. All grades of propane come in the form of raw material (refined crude oil or natural gas) and are stored in pressurized tanks and cylinders. Under pressure, propane is in a liquid state, and it turns to gas immediately after exiting its tank. It's colorless and odorless, which is why odorants are added to warn us if there are leaks. It's important to position tanks upright to prevent leakage, and generally, to follow instructions for use listed on the tank.

Propane is said to be harmless if inhaled by humans or animals, if spilled on the ground, or introduced to drinking water or freshwater and saltwater ecosystems. However, its volatile temperature characteristics (it has a boiling point of 44°F) make it harmful if it comes into direct contact with skin.

Check the make and brand of your grill to see if the manufacturer sells compatible fuel. You can opt for smaller propane containers, such as 1-pound cylinders that are sold for as low as $4 apiece.

Most camp stoves indicate how much fuel you'll need based on burn time. For example, a two-burner Coleman Classic Propane Stove with a 16.4-ounce propane cylinder will last for 60 minutes on high heat. A MSR Whisperlight Stove with 20 ounces of white gas will last 136 minutes (the heat setting does not vary). Total the cooking time in your recipes to help determine how much fuel you'll need. For example, if you plan to make three meals that require a total of 50 minutes cooking time at medium heat, a 16.4-ounce propane cylinder will be plenty. Depending on your stove, you may be able to buy an adapter for attaching to a larger propane tank (such as 5 or 10 gallons) on longer trips. Once empty, don't throw away the tank or cylinder; refill or exchange it at a gas station, garden center, hardware store, or outdoor store.

**Tip:** To position your camp stove or portable grill, find an open area without low-hanging branches that could catch on fire. Place your camp stove or portable grill on a flat space that's been cleared of brush and other loose debris that could catch fire.

In the United States, the 1990 amendments to the Clean Air Act favored propane as a fuel alternative to gasoline and diesel because it burns cleaner, with fewer emissions, and, thus, less air pollution. My bottom line? Propane is a petroleum-based product that must be used cautiously and sparingly in any scenario, especially in the outdoors.

# lighting a charcoal grill

The alchemy of cooking food over fire is what makes grilling—and camping—one of humankind's greatest pastimes. Wood smoke adds flavor to food that can't be replicated in other ways.

When it comes to lighting charcoal (see "Charcoal 101," page 26), I'm not a fan of lighter fluid; it adds a toxic flavor to food that defeats the purpose of cooking over charcoal. If you must use it, place a small pile of charcoal in the base of your grill and douse it with lighter fluid. Set it on fire, carefully, with matches or a lighter. When the coals are glowing red, rake the pile to one side with a grill brush.

A much better and surefire way to light your charcoal is with a chimney starter, which is inexpensive, durable, and simple to use. It means you'll have to lug it with you, but it will make the fire-building process easy, clean, and rewarding. Directions on how to use one follow.

1   Stuff a few wads of newspaper in the bottom of the chimney, beneath the metal grate. This compartment also keeps stray ash from scattering in the wind.

2   Stand the chimney upright and fill the cylinder with charcoal, preferably lump hardwood (see page 26).

3   Light the newspaper with matches or a lighter. The flames will carry upward to the charcoal.

4   When the flames have settled and the coals are glowing red and covered in gray ash, about 15 minutes, use welding gloves to pour the coals onto one side of the grill base to create a two-zone grilling setup (see page 27).

5   Place the hot, empty chimney out of reach of animals and children, and make sure grown-ups are aware of it too.

## charcoal 101

I always use hardwood lump charcoal, which is pure wood that's already been burned into charcoal chunks. It will give you a head start on the cooking process and impart a rich, wood-smoke flavor to your food. It's comparably priced to the more popular charcoal briquettes, which are made with compressed sawdust, wood scraps, coal dust, borax, limestone, sodium nitrate, and petroleum binders—none of which I want to add to my meal. Hardwood lump charcoal also burns faster than briquettes—a chimney's worth will be ready to use in 15 to 20 minutes. Most of the recipes in this book can be made with one chimney of charcoal, but have a second chimney ready to fire up for recipes with longer cooking times or if you're preparing multiple dishes at once.

## how to squelch a grease fire

Grease fires happen when fat, oil, or grease get hot enough to ignite. Outdoors, this is most likely to happen when fat drips onto the coals from food on the grill. If a grease fire erupts when you're with a crowd, everyone suddenly has an opinion on how to put it out, and chaos can escalate. Ask everyone to move to safety, and follow these do's and don'ts.

- Do turn off a fuel source, like propane, if you can safely reach the knob.

- Do stifle the flow of oxygen, like closing a lid, if possible.

- Do give the grease fire (if it's a manageable size) some time to burn off and subside.

- Do throw baking soda over the top of the fire (if is out of control) to snuff it out.

- Do not, I repeat, do NOT throw water on a grease fire. This will feed it.

- Do not swat at or attempt to cover the fire with a towel or clothing; this can cause fat to splatter on you and cause severe burning.

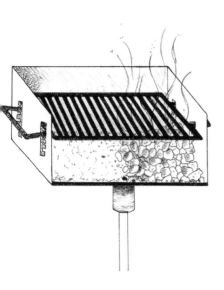

## two-zone grilling

Two-zone grilling is a process by which you create two cooking zones: low and high heat. This is accomplished by banking the coals on one side of the grill base, leaving the other side empty. The section of the grill grate directly over the coals is the hottest, usually used for searing and charring food. The low-temperature zone is best for slow-cooking over indirect heat, and also serves as a safety zone where you can move food to prevent it from burning, manage flare-ups, and keep food warm once cooked. Though it's referred to as two-zone setup, you inevitably end up with a third, medium-temperature cooking zone between the two.

## cooking with wood chips

When camping trips don't involve a campfire to cook over, wood chips can impart the same juicy, smoky flavors and color. If you're using a portable grill with a lid, the wood chips will transform your grill into a smoker, cooking your food in a fraction of the time. You can find wood chips online or at your local hardware store. When shopping, you're likely to come across wood chunks and wood pellets but I implore you to stick with wood chips. They're the most manageable, quicker to smoke, and give a true wood-fired flavor to your food. The most popular wood chips are apple, cherry, oak, mesquite, hickory, alder, maple, and pecan.

Here's how to use wood chips.

1 | Soak the wood chips in water for about 30 minutes. Drain before using.

2 | Fire your grill to the temperature specified in the recipe.

3 | Place the wood chips on top of the hot coals. When the wood chips begin smoking, start cooking.

4 | If using a grill with a lid, close the lid as soon as possible to capture the smoke, and keep it closed until the last second of cooking time.

# before
# you go

Whether you're heading to the local park or back-packing in the wild, food planning is key. You'll want to be thorough and even a bit lavish; there's no sense in forgoing nourishing, delicious meals at camp! I learned this when training as an outdoor guide in college, when I would make my own trail mix in my dorm room before heading out for the weekend. But without a kitchen, I couldn't prepare some of my favorite staples from scratch. During my first Fall Break home, I took over my mother's kitchen, experimenting with dense, homemade energy bars and condiments like ketchup and mustard. I made enough to bring back for my fellow trainees, all of whom welcomed the upgrade on our usual trail fare.

While the majority of the dishes in this book can be cooked outside, this section includes condiments, snacks, and treats that will enrich your camping experience and are great to have on hand when you arrive. And I promise, life will never be the same after roasting a homemade marshmallow over the campfire.

# BEST KETCHUP ON EARTH

PREP: 5 minutes
COOK: 1¼ hours
YIELD: 2 cups

One 750-gram box strained tomatoes
½ cup minced white onion
½ cup apple cider vinegar
⅓ cup maple syrup
2 teaspoons molasses
1½ teaspoons kosher salt
1 teaspoon grated garlic

This ketchup is everything you've been looking for. It's tangy, sweet, and rich! Most important, this recipe is preservative-free and made with natural sweeteners, so you can feel good about putting it on anything as well as serving it to your kids. My favorite brand of strained tomatoes is Pomi, which you can substitute with a 28-ounce can of pureed tomatoes, preferably Italian.

1   In a medium pot, combine all of the ingredients and stir together with a wooden spoon. Bring the mixture to a slow boil, then lower to a simmer and cook, stirring and scraping the bottom of the pot every 10 to 15 minutes, until the sauce reduces by half, about 1 hour; it should thickly coat the back of a spoon. Remove from the heat and let cool.

2   In a blender or with an immersion blender, whiz until the ketchup is silky smooth.

3   Store in a lidded glass jar or squeeze bottle in the refrigerator for up to 1 week.

Once you've made your own mustard, you'll be hard-pressed to buy it again. It's so dang easy, and it's fun to experiment with creating different flavors! It does require a tiny bit of patience, as the mustard seeds need about two days to soak. Try swapping the apple cider vinegar with other vinegars, pickle juice, or red or white wine.

# WHOLE-GRAIN HONEY MUSTARD

PREP: 5 minutes
COOK: None
YIELD: 1¼ cups

1   In an airtight container, combine the mustard seeds, mustard powder, and salt and stir with a fork. Add the beer, honey, and vinegar and stir to combine. Seal and let the mixture sit in a dark place at room temperature for at least 2 days or up to 3 days.

2   Transfer the mixture to a blender and whiz until it's a coarse consistency with some visible whole grains. The mustard will be spicy; for less heat and more sweetness, stir in up to 2 tablespoons honey.

3   Store in an airtight container in the refrigerator for up to 6 months.

½ cup yellow mustard seeds

2 tablespoons mustard powder

1 teaspoon kosher salt

½ cup pilsner beer, hard cider, or water

¼ cup honey, or as needed

3 tablespoons apple cider vinegar

# EASY ITALIAN MAYONNAISE

PREP: 7 minutes

COOK: None

YIELD: 1 cup

1 cup olive oil

1 egg yolk

2 tablespoons freshly squeezed lemon juice

½ teaspoon kosher salt

The mayonnaise I grew up with was an entirely different breed than store-bought American mayonnaise. Italian mayonnaise relies on a bright-yellow egg yolk, olive oil, lemon juice, and salt—that's it! It tastes pure and rich and makes the perfect base for flavored aioli, which is simply mayonnaise with garlic. It's also delicious smeared on bread with fresh tomatoes, fresh herbs, and a sprinkle of salt and pepper. For a lighter version, substitute ⅓ cup of the olive oil with safflower oil.

1   In a blender, combine ¼ cup of the olive oil, the egg yolk, lemon juice, and salt. Put the remaining ¾ cup olive oil in a liquid measuring cup with a spout and get ready to meditate! With the blender on low speed, slowly drizzle in the oil in an extremely thin stream—this should take about 5 minutes. Once there is about ¼ cup olive oil remaining in the measuring cup and the mayonnaise in the blender is visibly emulsified (thick and smooth in consistency), you can pick up your pouring speed. (If the final mayonnaise is too thick, thin it out with a little bit of warm water.)

2   Store in an airtight container in the refrigerator for up to 1 month.

## VARIATIONS

For Curry Aioli, add 1 peeled and grated garlic clove and 1 teaspoon curry powder along with the salt and proceed as directed.

For Smoked Paprika Aioli, add 1 peeled and grated garlic clove and 1 teaspoon smoked paprika along with the salt and proceed as directed.

This deceivingly simple dip is a staple in my outdoor kitchen, combining olive oil with a spice mix based on the enchanting Middle Eastern za'atar. The spice mix alone will make any dish sing; try scattering it over grilled vegetables and meat or a simple salad. Even better: dunk Charred Bread (page 102) into this dip; you may need help picking up your jaw from the floor. It is amazing, or as my friends say, *emm-a-ZING*! I also love frying eggs in 2 tablespoons of the dip; they develop a crispy, sesame-herb underlayer that will make your eyes roll back in your head with glee. For a thicker dip or spreadable paste, add more Zesty Za'atar to the olive oil. This recipe makes 1 cup za'atar, enough to stock the pantry; in a birthday pinch, you can pack a small gift jar.

1   To make the za'atar: Using a Microplane, finely grate the zest from the lemons. Fresh lemon zest clumps together, so spread it out on a plate to dry for 15 to 20 minutes before mixing with the remaining ingredients.

2   In a food processor or blender, combine the lemon zest, sesame seeds, thyme, rosemary, oregano, and salt and pulse until everything is incorporated and the herbs are ground. You can continue grinding the seasoning into a fine powder, depending on your preference for texture. (If you do not have a food processor or blender, mince fresh herbs with a sharp chef's knife or crumble dried herbs with your fingers before combining the ingredients.) Transfer the seasoning to a lidded jar and store in a cool, dark place for up to 3 months.

3   In a small bowl, combine the olive oil with a heaping 2 tablespoons za'atar and stir to mix. Transfer the dip to a lidded jar or airtight container.

4   Store at room temperature for up to 24 hours.

# ZESTY ZA'ATAR OLIVE OIL DIP

PREP: 20 minutes
COOK: None
YIELD: ½ cup

### ZESTY ZA'ATAR

2 lemons

1 cup toasted sesame seeds

½ cup fresh thyme leaves, or ¼ cup dried

¼ cup fresh rosemary leaves, or 2 tablespoons dried

2 tablespoons fresh oregano or marjoram leaves, or 1 teaspoon dried (or a mix)

¼ cup coarse sea salt (preferably sel gris)

½ cup extra-virgin olive oil

Note: I like to start with fresh herbs and dry them myself for a more vibrant flavor and a longer-lasting spice mix. Gather your herbs into small bundles and tie off the stems with kitchen twine. Hang them upside down from a nail or a string tied across your doorframe, away from direct sunlight, and let them dry for 5 to 10 days. Strip the leaves to use and then compost the stems.

# CLASSIC CREAMY HUMMUS

PREP: 10 minutes

COOK: None

YIELD: 6 to 8 servings

Two 15-ounce cans garbanzo beans, drained and rinsed

1 cup extra-virgin olive oil, plus more for drizzling

¼ cup tahini

Juice of 2 lemons

3 garlic cloves, peeled, or to taste

1 teaspoon kosher salt

½ teaspoon paprika (optional)

1 tablespoon finely chopped fresh parsley (optional)

It's rare that we get to taste a homemade version of this Mediterranean dip, which is surprising because it's so easy to make. Once you get the basic recipe down, you can play with additions like pesto, sun-dried tomatoes, or even curry! If hummus makes you gassy, be sure to give the beans a thorough rinse and rub them together with a kitchen towel to remove the skins. If using the hummus as an ingredient in a sandwich (see page 76) or other recipe, leave off the garnish, which is primarily for presentation. If serving as a dip, keep the container upright in the cooler; it will have (almost) the same presentation when you open it up at camp. Serve with Charred Bread (page 102), sliced fresh vegetables, or a selection of cheeses and cured meats.

1   In a blender, combine the garbanzo beans, olive oil, tahini, lemon juice, garlic, and salt and whiz until creamy and smooth. Transfer to a shallow airtight container. Drizzle with olive oil and dust with the paprika and parsley, if desired.

2   Seal the container and then chill for up to 7 days.

I can always count on my friend Elizabeth to bring this starter to a potluck; it's a simple dish she learned while working with fishermen in Alaska's wild salmon country. Smoking salmon is a method of preserving it, making it ideal for camping and fishing trips and an extraordinary replacement to the more traditional lox whipped with cream cheese. For extra zing, I add lemon zest and a medley of fresh herbs. My favorite combination is 1 tablespoon tarragon and 1 tablespoon chives (technically an allium but used like an herb). If you're harvesting your own chives or buying them from the farmers' market, track down a few purple chive blossoms for garnish. My favorite smoked salmon is Alaska Gold brand, which you can buy online from the fisher(wo)men and keep on hand in the freezer. By preparing this at home, you arrive with it ready-made for quick satisfaction, like smearing on bagels or Charred Bread (page 102). If you're bypassing the capers, try topping your spread with Quick Pickles (page 38); a bright, tangy burst helps cut through this rich dip. For a lighter snack, serve it as a dip with raw vegetables.

1  In a medium bowl, use a fork to beat together the cream cheese and yogurt until smooth and spreadable.

2  Break up the smoked salmon with the fork or your fingers and add it to the cream cheese mixture, stirring together until incorporated. Stir in the herbs, lemon zest, lemon juice, and capers (if using) and season with pepper.

3  Store in an airtight container, chilled, for up to 5 days.

# SMOKED SALMON SPREAD

PREP: 7 minutes

COOK: None

YIELD: 4 to 6 servings

---

One 8-ounce block cream cheese (see Note)

3 tablespoons plain yogurt

4 ounces smoked salmon (preferably wild caught)

2 tablespoons minced fresh herbs (such as tarragon, thyme, oregano, basil, chives, or a combination)

1 tablespoon finely grated lemon zest, plus 1½ teaspoons freshly squeezed lemon juice

1 tablespoon capers, rinsed if packed in salt (optional)

Freshly ground black pepper

Note: It helps to bring the cream cheese to room temperature, but if you're making this in a pinch, you can still whip cold, cubed cream cheese with a little extra elbow grease.

# QUICK PICKLES

PREP: 5 minutes

COOK: None

YIELD: One 8-ounce jar

---

1 cup apple cider vinegar, or as needed

2 tablespoons honey

1 tablespoon kosher salt

Vegetables of your choice (see below)

Quick pickles have several benefits. You don't have to wait for the fermentation process, and they can add a tart crunch to any dish within minutes of making them. Even better, they last for a couple of months in the fridge, continuing to evolve in flavor. And above all, vinegar and salt are natural preservatives, making quick pickles travel-worthy condiments that belong at camp. Here's my basic pickle brine and suggested vegetables to use. You can also play with flavor variations, such as adding 2 garlic cloves, 1 teaspoon mustard seeds, and ½ teaspoon dill seed to the jar when brining.

---

1   In an 16-ounce jar, combine the vinegar, honey, and salt. Shake vigorously to incorporate

2   Pack your prepared vegetable(s) into the jar, making sure they are submerged in the brine. If the vegetables aren't covered, add more vinegar as needed. Seal the jar tightly and shake again to incorporate any added vinegar.

3   Chill for at least 10 minutes, or up to 2 months, before serving.

Note: To make an assortment of pickles, use one-fourth of the suggested volume of each vegetable and pack all of them together.

| VEGETABLE | QUANTITY | PREPARATION |
|-----------|----------|-------------|
| Carrot | 3 or 4 medium | Peel and cut into ⅛-inch slices or matchsticks (if organic, no need to peel) |
| Cucumber | 1 large | Cut into ⅛-inch slices, wedges, or matchsticks |
| Radish | 5 or 6 medium | Trim and compost tops and roots and cut into ⅛-inch slices |
| Red Onion | 1 large | Halve and slice thinly |

It wasn't until I moved to the heart of maple country in Ithaca, New York, that I truly appreciated maple syrup. I remember my first sap boil at the Sapsquatch Sugar Shack, where my friends kept warm with song and maple-laced whiskey. When I dipped my finger into a bucket of clear tree juice, just collected from the forest, it tasted remarkably crisp, like melted ice, and faintly sweet. The bucket was then poured into an enormous metal tray over a roaring fire, where the juice boiled down to amber syrup. Days later, when my friend Elizabeth brought this sweet-and-salty trail mix to a potluck, I was hardly surprised. At the end of a long, stark winter, the taste of maple is like liquid sunshine celebrating spring's imminent arrival. This trail mix couldn't be easier to make. Pack smaller portions in ziplock bags for an instant soul-booster on the trail.

1   Preheat the oven to 350°F. Line a rimmed baking sheet with parchment paper.

2   In a large bowl, combine the almonds, maple syrup, olive oil, rosemary, and salt. Spread the mixture in a single layer on the prepared baking sheet and roast for 5 minutes. Remove from the oven, toss the almonds, spread in a single layer again, and continue to roast until dark brown, 7 minutes more. Don't let the almonds burn!

3   Remove from the oven and stir in the raisins so they absorb the oil and the flavor of the rosemary. Spread the mixture into a single layer again and let cool completely.

4   Store in an airtight container or ziplock bag in a cool, dark place for up to 1 month.

# MAPLE-ROSEMARY ROASTED ALMOND MIX

PREP: 10 minutes
COOK: 12 minutes
YIELD: 3½ cups

2½ cups raw almonds

1 tablespoon maple syrup

1 tablespoon olive oil

1 tablespoon chopped fresh rosemary

1 teaspoon coarse sea salt (preferably sel gris)

1 cup raisins

# FIRELIGHT QUINOA GRANOLA CLUSTERS

PREP: 15 minutes

COOK: About 45 minutes

YIELD: About 8 cups

---

½ cup quinoa, toasted (see Note)

4 cups rolled oats

1½ cups unsweetened coconut chips

½ cup sesame seeds

½ cup sunflower seeds

2 tablespoons flaxseeds

2 teaspoons ground cinnamon

1 teaspoon ground cardamom

½ cup olive oil

½ cup maple syrup

½ cup honey

1½ teaspoons vanilla extract

¾ cup dried cranberries or other dried fruit (optional)

Note: Quinoa has a bitter coating called saponin. Nowadays, most quinoa is prerinsed to remove the saponin, but to maximize flavor and be sure it's not bitter, follow these steps:

In a pan over medium heat, toast the quinoa until they start popping and smell roasted, 5 to 8 minutes. Then, rinse in a fine-mesh strainer before using.

I've sampled hundreds of granolas across the world and baked even more batches in my kitchen. None compare to this recipe, which I developed for Firelight Camps. When I eat granola, I dig for the clusters, and this is a whole batch of clusters! Pack this as a perfect fireside cereal with fresh fruit and yogurt, or for energizing morsels on the trail. Play with seasonal variations, like lemon zest and dried strawberries in summer, or extra cinnamon and apple chips in autumn.

---

1   Position two racks in the center and lower third of the oven and preheat to 350°F. Line two large, rimmed baking sheets with parchment paper.

2   In a large bowl, stir together the quinoa, oats, coconut chips, sesame seeds, sunflower seeds, flaxseeds, cinnamon, and cardamom. In a medium bowl, whisk together the olive oil, maple syrup, honey, and vanilla. Pour the wet ingredients into the dry ingredients and stir together until combined.

3   Spread the mixture evenly onto the prepared baking sheets, flattening it with the back of a spatula.

4   Place the baking sheets on the prepared oven racks and bake for 20 minutes. Remove the sheets from the oven and toss and redistribute the granola with a spatula to help it brown evenly. Flatten it again—hard! Return the granola to the oven, switching the sheets to ensure both are cooked evenly, and continue to bake until toasted brown, 20 minutes.

5   Remove from the oven and sprinkle the cranberries (if using) over the top of the warm granola. Let the granola cool completely, 15 to 20 minutes. Do not break it up earlier or you'll lose those precious clusters! Once cooled, break the granola into smaller clusters and transfer to an airtight container or ziplock bag.

6   Store in a cool, dark place for up to 1 month.

# NO-BAKE CHOCOLATE PRETZEL POWER BARS

PREP: 7 minutes

FREEZE: 20 minutes

YIELD: 20 bars

---

1½ cups honey

6 cups rolled oats

20 dates, pitted and chopped

1 cup thin pretzel sticks, broken into ½-inch pieces, plus ½ cup crushed pretzel sticks

¾ cup unsalted raw or roasted peanuts

1 cup chocolate chips, plus 2 tablespoons

1 teaspoon sunflower oil or coconut oil

For my twin sister's bachelorette party, we traded in heels for hiking boots and hit the trails of New York's Mohonk Preserve. I brought along a batch of these raw, naturally sweetened granola bars to keep us going. This is a play on a recipe my childhood friend's mom used to make, which we would gobble down after running around outside all day. They are a nourishing no-bake treat that invites variation. Not a pretzel fan? Add raisins instead! You won't hit the trails again without one of these stashed in your pack. While best stored chilled, these hold up at ambient temperature, though the chocolate will be prone to melting.

---

1   In a small pot over low heat, warm the honey until it reaches the consistency of thin syrup.

2   In a food processor or blender, combine the oats, dates, and honey and whiz until a sticky, grainy batter forms.

3   Transfer the oat mixture to a large bowl. Add the pretzel pieces and peanuts and mix together with your hands or a sturdy spoon. Refrigerate for 5 to 10 minutes to cool, then stir in the 1 cup chocolate chips. (If you add the chocolate chips to the batter while it's still warm, they will melt and create a more heavenly, chocolaty bar— your call!)

4   Line a rimmed baking sheet with aluminum foil and lightly grease with the sunflower oil.

5   Transfer the batter to the prepared baking sheet and use a rolling pin or empty wine bottle to roll out into a slab about ½ inch thick. (If the batter sticks, dust the rolling pin with gluten-free flour.) Sprinkle the remaining 2 tablespoons chocolate chips and the crushed pretzels over the top and roll gently over the surface to press into the batter.

6   Freeze the batter for 20 minutes. Using a sharp knife, cut into twenty rectangular bars (or any other size desired). Cover each bar individually with aluminum foil or plastic wrap.

7   Store in an airtight container, chilled, for up to 2 weeks.

One summer in college, I worked with the Food & Agriculture Organization in Kenya. I stayed with my uncle in Nairobi, home to a booming Indian population. After work, we would jog to his neighbor's house to stock up on my favorite Indian treats. When she opened the door, the strong smell of curry gripped me by the nose and dragged me into her kitchen, a blue-and-white-tiled room flooded with sunlight and lined with wooden shelves. She would pull down jars of chutney, candied ginger, and a spicy snack mix, which I always packed to tide me over on all-day farm visits. On one field trip, we punctured a tire and, try as we might, could not remove the rusted bolts to swap the spare. Six hours passed without signs of help, and we'd long since demolished my snack mix. Just as the sun was setting, we heard footsteps approaching through the brush. We stifled squeals of joy not wanting to scare off our saviors, but were quickly subdued with awe as two hulking elephants traipsed in front of us. Eventually a car passed by and helped us, but the wait had been well worth my first encounter with elephants in the wild. Make time to prepare these bars before heading to camp; you'll be grateful to have them for whatever adventure lies ahead!

# WILD ELEPHANT SNACK BARS

PREP: 25 minutes
COOK: 20 minutes
YIELD: 8 bars

---

1½ cups rolled oats

¼ cup puffed brown rice cereal

½ cup unsweetened banana chips

½ cup unsalted roasted peanuts or cashew pieces, coarsely chopped

¼ cup dried mango, dried pineapple, or candied ginger, or a combination

2 tablespoons oat flour or brown rice flour

1 teaspoon curry powder

½ teaspoon ground turmeric

¼ teaspoon ground ginger

¼ teaspoon baking soda

¼ teaspoon fine salt

⅓ cup honey

2 tablespoons coconut oil, melted

1   Preheat the oven to 350°F. Line a 9-inch square baking pan with parchment paper or grease with oil.

2   In a large bowl, combine the oats, rice cereal, banana chips, peanuts, dried mango, oat flour, curry powder, turmeric, ginger, baking soda, and salt. In a small bowl, whisk together the honey and coconut oil. Pour the wet ingredients into the dry ingredients and stir together until combined.

3   Transfer the mixture to the prepared baking pan, using the back of a spatula to flatten with all your might. Did you press down hard enough? Good. Now use the palms of your hands to press down even harder.

4   Bake for 15 minutes, then check to see if the bars are toasted brown. You may need to cook for 5 minutes more. Remove from the oven and let cool completely in the pan. Using a sharp knife, cut into eight rectangular bars (or smaller pieces if desired). Cover each bar individually with aluminum foil or plastic wrap.

5   Store in an airtight container in a cool, dark place for up to 2 weeks, or chilled for up to 1 month.

# HONEY GRAHAM CRACKERS

PREP: 20 minutes
COOK: 18 minutes
YIELD: 20 crackers

---

¾ cup plus 1 tablespoon unsalted butter, at room temperature

⅓ cup packed dark brown sugar

¼ cup granulated sugar

1 teaspoon honey

1¼ cups unbleached all-purpose flour

1 cup whole-wheat flour

½ teaspoon baking soda

½ teaspoon fine salt

¼ teaspoon ground cinnamon

½ teaspoon coarse sea salt (optional)

Note: To make a s'mores banana boat, slit a banana ½ inch deep, lengthwise, leaving the stem and bottom intact. Open the peel to form a pocket and then stuff with crushed graham crackers, chopped marshmallows, and chocolate chips. Wrap in aluminum foil and place over medium coals for 5 to 10 minutes. Serve hot.

Graham flour was named after Reverend Sylvester Graham, a nineteenth-century Presbyterian minister. He preached the importance of whole-grain bread during the Industrial Revolution, when white bread—made with flour stripped of its nutrients—became a phenomenon. Fascinating, right? As a whole-foods aficionado myself, this recipe honors its roots by using whole-wheat flour, which is more easily found than graham flour, and dark brown sugar, which gives it a subtle molasses flavor and darker color. Extra butter imparts the richness and supple texture of a shortbread cookie, so your s'more won't crumble on the first bite. A tape measure is helpful for cutting traditionally shaped crackers, but you can eyeball the measurements, adjust the size, or use any shaped cookie cutter! These crackers are also excellent as a snack, dunked into coffee or Hot Chocolatada (page 183), or served with soft cheese. Save the border scraps for crumbling over Old-Fashioned Bourbon Fool with Cherries (page 173) or a s'mores banana boat (see Note). For a salty-sweet finish, try the coarse sea salt garnish; it takes these crackers to another level, especially sandwiched around chocolate.

---

1   Preheat the oven to 350°F. Cut two 17-inch pieces of parchment paper.

2   In the bowl of a stand mixer fitted with the paddle attachment, combine the butter, brown sugar, and granulated sugar and mix on low speed for about 30 seconds, until incorporated. Stop the mixer, add the honey, and turn to medium speed, whipping for about 8 minutes.

3   In a medium bowl, combine the all-purpose flour, whole-wheat flour, baking soda, fine salt, and cinnamon and stir with a fork to incorporate.

4   When the butter and sugar have formed a caramel-colored paste, stop the mixer and scrape down the sides of the bowl with a spatula. Start the mixture on low speed and slowly add the dry ingredients until incorporated. Then, turn the speed to medium-low and mix until the dough comes together, about 30 seconds; it will look like crumbly, wet sand. Turn off the mixer and scrape down the sides of the bowl.

5   Turn out the dough onto one of the pieces of parchment paper. Collect the dough between the palms of your hands, squeeze firmly to press into a smooth ball, and knead for about 30 seconds. Flatten the dough into a 6 by 8-inch rectangle, about 1 inch thick.

6   Place the second piece of parchment on top of the dough and, using a rolling pin, roll into a rough 15 by 12-inch rectangle (with irregular edges), about ¼ inch thick. (Recycle the top piece of parchment paper or store in the freezer for future recipes.)

7   Using a knife or pizza cutter, trim a 1-inch border from the longer sides of the rectangle, and 1½ inches from the shorter sides. Save the scraps to bake. Working with the longer side of the rectangle, make horizontal cuts every 2½ inches, yielding four rows. Working with the shorter side of the rectangle, make vertical cuts every 2½ inches, yielding five columns and making twenty squares. Prick each square with a fork or toothpick to form two dotted rows on each side of the dividing line. Carefully slide the parchment paper with the dough (and scraps) onto a 12 by 17-inch rimmed baking sheet. Sprinkle with the coarse sea salt, if desired.

8   Bake until the edges are lightly browned, about 18 minutes, rotating the baking sheet halfway through to ensure even baking.

9   While the crackers are still warm in the pan, cut along the original lines and use a spatula to transfer (with the scraps) to a wire rack and let cool completely, about 15 minutes.

10  Store in an airtight container at room temperature for up to 1 week.

Though s'mores are an American creation, the marshmallow itself dates back to ancient Egypt, when sap from the mallow plant (*Althaea officinalis*) was sweetened with honey to cure sore throats. I love this connection to medicine in the wild. While marshmallows may not serve the same medicinal benefits today, they provide infinite outdoor happiness, and *that* is arguably the best medicine! Months before we opened Firelight Camps, I set out to create marshmallows from scratch; ones that would puff up and torch over the fire in true form. I discovered this could be accomplished only with corn syrup, as marshmallows made with alternative sweeteners and egg whites are lovely but melt miserably off the stick and into the fire. It's best to make marshmallows on a low-humidity day, so the sugar can adequately dry out. (I've even left them in an air-conditioned room overnight!) You can also play with other extracts, like almond, lemon, and strawberry, combined with a few drops of natural food coloring to match the flavor.

1 Grease a 9 by 13-inch baking pan with the sunflower oil, making sure to get the sides.

2 In a medium bowl, combine the powdered sugar and cornstarch and stir to mix. Sift ½ cup of the powdered sugar–cornstarch mixture into the prepared pan, coating the bottom. (Sifting the mixture will prevent hard chunks on the surface of your marshmallows.) Reserve the remaining sugar mixture.

3 In a heatproof bowl or the insert of a double boiler, combine the ½ cup cold water and gelatin.

4 Meanwhile, in a medium pot, combine the granulated sugar, corn syrup, honey, and remaining ⅓ cup water. To prevent sugar crystals from forming, gently stir the ingredients to incorporate, or better yet, swirl the pot without splashing the mixture on the sides. Place over medium heat and cook to 252°F, about 12 minutes; use a candy thermometer to check the temperature. If the mixture begins to rise and foam, stir gently a few times. Transfer the mixture to the bowl of a stand mixer fitted with the whip attachment and allow to cool to 212°F, about 10 minutes.

continued

# HEAVENLY VANILLA MARSH-MALLOWS

PREP: 10 minutes
COOK: About 15 minutes
SET: Overnight
YIELD: 48 marshmallows

---

1 teaspoon sunflower oil

1¼ cups powdered sugar

1¼ cups cornstarch

½ cup water, cold, plus ⅓ cup

2 tablespoons powdered gelatin

2 cups plus 2 tablespoons granulated sugar

½ cup light corn syrup

3 tablespoons honey

2 teaspoons vanilla extract

5   Meanwhile, fill a small saucepan or the bottom of the double boiler with 1 inch of water and bring to a simmer over medium-low heat. Place the hydrated gelatin over the water bath and swirl with a spoon until it reaches liquid form, about 3 minutes. Turn off the heat and let cool.

6   Turn the stand mixer to low speed and add the vanilla and liquid gelatin. Gradually increase the mixer speed to high (take about 30 seconds) and whip for 8 minutes, until the mixture is quadrupled in volume and well aerated. When you stop the mixer, the marshmallow should stand up in stiff peaks and hold its shape rather than flow down the sides of the mixing bowl.

7   Using a spatula, quickly scrape the marshmallow into the middle of the prepared pan; you'll have a big sticky mound. Work fast! It will be very sticky and you will not be able to scoop every last bit out of the mixing bowl and whip attachment. Sift ¼ cup powdered sugar–cornstarch mixture over the top and then use your hands or the back of a spatula to spread the marshmallow evenly in the pan, patting down to create a flat surface. (If using your hands, you may need to coat with additional sugar powder.)

8   Cover with aluminum foil or plastic wrap and let stand overnight in a cool, dry place.

9   Grease a knife and slide it down the edges of the marshmallow to separate from the pan. Turn onto a cutting board and cut the marshmallows into 48 squares (eight columns and six rows). Toss the marshmallows in the bowl with the remaining sugar mixture, turning to coat all sides so they are no longer sticky.

10  Transfer the marshmallows to an airtight container or ziplock bag and store at room temperature for up to 1 month.

Every Christmas, our thirty-person White Elephant gift exchange ends in a hot pursuit for my mom's banana bread. People hide it under their chairs or in their coats, hoping that the next person will forget it's still up for grabs. Luckily, after the holiday winds down, my mom always sends me and my siblings home with our own loaves. This is how I discovered it was the ultimate on-the-go treat and worth preparing before hitting the road. Not only is this a foolproof recipe for sweetening any outdoor gathering, this is also the first time it's been shared beyond our family (thank you, Mamma!). Plan ahead! The secret to this bread is using previously frozen, extra-ripe bananas. Also, mini chocolate chips work best because they are lighter and stay suspended in the batter, but you can substitute regular chocolate chips if that's what you have on hand. For a decadent PB&J, I like to use banana bread in place of regular bread. Serve warm or at room temperature.

1   Preheat the oven to 350°F. Butter and flour two 8 by 4-inch loaf pans.

2   In the bowl of a stand mixer, combine the sugar and butter and beat until smooth and creamy. Beat in the eggs, one at a time, until incorporated, then beat in the bananas. In a separate bowl, stir together the flour, baking soda, and salt. Using a spatula, fold the flour mixture into the banana mixture until incorporated.

3   In a small bowl, toss the chocolate chips with a spoonful of flour (this will help them stay suspended in the batter). Fold the chocolate chips and walnuts (if using) into the batter until evenly distributed. Divide the batter between the prepared loaf pans.

4   Bake the loaves until a toothpick inserted into the center comes out clean, about 60 minutes. Remove from the oven and let cool completely.

5   Store covered in plastic wrap at ambient temperature for up to 1 week, or freeze for up to 3 months (especially handy for emergency chocolate cravings).

# MAMMA'S FAMOUS CHOCOLATE CHIP–BANANA BREAD

PREP: 25 minutes
COOK: 60 minutes
YIELD: 2 loaves

2 cups sugar

¾ cup plus 2 tablespoons unsalted butter, room temperature

4 eggs

6 frozen bananas, thawed and mashed, or extremely ripe bananas

2½ cups unbleached all-purpose flour, plus more as needed

2 teaspoons baking soda

½ teaspoon fine salt

1 cup mini chocolate chips

½ cup chopped walnuts (optional)

# AYLA'S LEMON-OLIVE OIL THUMB-PRINTS

PREP: 10 minutes

COOK: 12 minutes

YIELD: 16 cookies

---

1½ cups almond flour

Finely grated zest of 1 lemon

⅛ teaspoon fine salt

¼ cup tahini

¼ cup honey

1 teaspoon olive oil

½ teaspoon vanilla extract

12 whole almonds or chocolate chips (optional)

Not long after my daughter, Ayla, started eating solids, she gummed a fresh-baked thumbprint cookie from our local grocery store. She loved it, so I set to making a less crumbly, travel-friendly version that we could take on hikes and road trips. This Italian-inspired thumbprint is one of the easiest, sweetest, nuttiest, protein-packed treats you'll ever come across. For little ones under the age of one year, swap the honey with maple syrup. If you're baking for a crowd, double or triple the recipe.

---

1   Preheat the oven to 350°F. Line a rimmed baking sheet with parchment paper.

2   In a large bowl, combine the almond flour, lemon zest, and salt. In a small bowl, whisk together the tahini, honey, olive oil, and vanilla. Pour the wet ingredients into the dry ingredients and stir well until combined. Use your hands to form the dough into a large ball.

3   Pinch off about 1 tablespoon of the dough at a time and roll into a small ball with the palms of your hands. Place on the prepared baking sheet and repeat with the remaining dough, spacing the balls 1 to 2 inches apart. Gently press your pinkie finger (or a toddler's thumb) into the center of each ball to lightly flatten the cookie until it is about ¾ inch thick. Don't worry too much about the shape; whether your version is flatter, thicker, or rounder, the cookies will be just as good! If desired, press an almond or chocolate chip into the center of each cookie.

4   Bake until the bottom edges of the cookies are toasted brown, 10 to 12 minutes. Transfer the cookies to a wire rack to cool.

5   Store in an airtight container at room temperature for up to 2 weeks (though I can promise you they won't last that long), or freeze for up to 3 months.

# BREAKFAST

If the birdsong doesn't draw you from your tent, these recipes will. This chapter is designed to help you create a quick meal or leisurely spread so you can kick off your adventure on the right foot.

# CARDAMOM-MINT TURKISH COFFEE

PREP: 2 minutes

COOK: 5 minutes

YIELD: 1 serving

---

¾ cup water

2 tablespoons ground coffee

1 cardamom pod, pod and seeds gently crushed with the back of a spoon

2 fresh mint leaves or ¼ teaspoon dried mint

Whole milk or other creamer for flavor

Raw honey for flavor

When I was in Istanbul, I discovered Turkish coffee, a gritty brew that charmed me with its cardamom spice. I was traveling with my twin sister and friends, and after many late nights of storytelling and hookah, we came to depend on this small, thunderous cup in the morning. The coffee was always prepared simply, with the same props you'd be able to find around a campfire. The ingredient proportions here are for a single serving and can be adapted to any method of brewing. I provide instructions for a pour-over (or dripper) device or using a pot on the stove top. For a pour-over device, you may need #4 coffee filters. For the stove top, you'll need a fine-mesh tea strainer. Don't skimp on the quality of your coffee; I like to grind beans the day before I head out, packing them in a ziplock bag. For a refreshing variation, let the coffee cool and then serve over ice.

---

1   In a small pot, bring the water to a boil and then remove from the heat.

2   *Pour-over method:* If using a coffee filter, rinse it with a splash of the hot water to remove the papery taste. Add the coffee, cardamom, and 1 mint leaf to the filter and pour in the water. Stir once and then let the coffee drip into a camper's mug.

*Stove-top method:* Add the coffee, cardamom, and 1 mint leaf to the pot of water, stir, and let steep for 4 minutes. Pour the coffee through a small fine-mesh strainer into a camper's mug.

3   Flavor your coffee by stirring in milk and honey. Gently bruise the remaining mint leaf with your fingers and add to your mug for aroma and garnish before serving.

Good-bye, oatmeal. Hello, quinoa breakfast bowl. Inspired by a recipe from cookbook author Heidi Swanson, this healthful, energizing, protein-rich breakfast masquerades as a decadent dish you'll want to eat all day! It's fun to set up a toppings buffet so each camper can make his or her own bowl. If traveling light, you can substitute dried fruit for fresh fruit. Bring a can of coconut milk, and save extra for adding to coffee or drizzling over Firelight Quinoa Granola Clusters (page 40).

**PREP** Preheat the oven to 325°F. On a rimmed baking sheet, toss together the nuts, coconut oil, and ¼ teaspoon of the salt and spread in a single layer. Toast in the oven until the nuts turn caramel brown, about 15 minutes. Transfer to a second baking sheet and let cool completely. Store in an airtight container or ziplock bag in a cool, dark place for up to 2 weeks.

1   Transfer the prepared nuts and the berries to small bowls with spoons for self-serving, or serve directly out of the containers.

2   In a medium pot, combine the quinoa, water, and ¾ cup of the coconut milk. Bring to a rolling boil over high heat, then cover the pot, turn the heat to low, and simmer for 12 minutes. Quickly uncover the pot and stir the quinoa to check if it's done; the liquid should be completely absorbed and the quinoa full and fluffy. If needed, continue to cook for 1 to 3 minutes more. Remove the pot from the heat and let stand for 5 minutes. Fluff the quinoa with a fork and cover the pot to keep warm.

3   Just before serving, drizzle the remaining ¼ cup coconut milk and the honey into the quinoa and stir to combine. Using a Microplane, grate lemon zest over the top and sprinkle with the remaining ½ teaspoon salt. Spoon into campers' bowls and let each camper top their quinoa with blueberries and toasted nuts. Store leftovers in an airtight container, chilled, for up to 5 days.

# COCONUT-QUINOA BREAKFAST BOWL WITH LEMON AND BLUEBERRIES

PREP: 10 minutes
COOK: 20 minutes
YIELD: 4 servings

½ cup coarsely chopped walnuts, almonds, hazelnuts, or a mix

1 tablespoon melted coconut oil

¾ teaspoon coarse sea salt (preferably sel gris)

1 cup fresh blueberries or other seasonal fruit

1 cup quinoa (see Note, page 40)

1¼ cups water

1 cup coconut milk (see Note, page 172)

2 tablespoons honey

1 lemon

# AMMA'S FRUIT SALAD WITH HONEY, LIME, AND MINT

PREP: 20 minutes

COOK: None

YIELD: 4 to 6 servings

---

1 pound fresh strawberries, stemmed and thinly sliced

Two 20-ounce cans pineapple chunks, drained

2 grapefruits, supremed (see Note)

¼ cup honey

Finely grated zest and juice of 2 limes

⅓ cup plus 1 tablespoon packed fresh mint leaves, thinly sliced

2 tablespoons cognac, or to taste (optional)

Note: To supreme a grapefruit, use a sharp paring knife to slice away the peel, pith, and translucent membrane. Hold the grapefruit over a bowl and carefully slice along the membrane that sandwiches each wedge, removing the juicy interior from the core. Catch the supremed wedges in the bowl. Squeeze the juice from the remaining core into a jar; add it to sparkling water with honey for a refreshing soda.

Even though my mother-in-law's family is Jewish, Christmas is their favorite holiday, and I'm sure it's because of this divine fruit salad. My husband's grandmother, Amma, was the first female certified metalsmith in the state of Pennsylvania, a jeweler and matriarch who was also a verified hoot. I've simplified Amma's recipe for quick assembly before heading out to camp. Peeling the grapefruit from its membrane is the only tedious, but wholly worthwhile, step, and it goes much faster with extra help. The salad becomes juicier over time, so prepare it at most a day in advance and pack into jars or sturdy bowls for serving. You can either portion out the cognac for this dish into a smaller bottle, or bring a whole bottle so you'll have extra for making hot toddies with Scorched Lemon-ade (page 92). You can substitute the canned pineapple with 4 cups of ½-inch cubes fresh pineapple, peeled and cored. This is about half a medium pineapple, so chop the rest for snacking at camp, or look for pre-cut fresh pineapple at your grocery store. Add leftovers to a Campari Sangria Spritz (page 94).

---

**PREP** Pack the strawberries, pineapple, and grapefruits in a large container. Strawberries tend to stain other food red, so if you want to preserve each fruit's color before assembling the salad, keep the fruit separated in sections or pack them in separate containers. Seal and then chill for up to 3 days.

In a small jar, combine the honey, lime zest, and lime juice; shake until mixed; and then chill for up to 3 days. Let come to ambient temperature before assembling the dish.

1   Transfer the strawberries, pineapple, and grapefruits to a large bowl (unless serving directly from the container). Gently mix in ⅓ cup of the mint, being careful not to crush the fruit. Pour the honey syrup over the fruit salad and gently toss. Add the cognac (if using) and gently toss again. Taste the salad and add more cognac as desired. (Beware: You may get a buzz in the tasting process.) Sprinkle the remaining 1 tablespoon sliced mint over the top.

2   Serve immediately. Store leftovers in an airtight container, chilled, for up to 3 days.

My first introduction to baked beans was remarkably far from any tent, but rather in Terminal 3 of London's Heathrow Airport. This was the first stop on family holidays to visit my grandparents. My three siblings and I could always count on the duty-free store to carry groaning shelves of Cadbury chocolate Flakes, Jelly Babies, and Fruit Pastilles, which were the last thing my mother wanted us to have after a sleepless red-eye. Instead, she herded us into the nearest restaurant for sausages and baked beans. Baked beans are a camping staple because they're a one-can dish, already packed with seasoning. But try this homemade version, which eclipses the canned kind while keeping it simple. If using a chunky marinara sauce, puree it in a blender until smooth. Serve alongside Bird in a Nest with Honeyed Avo (page 68).

**PREP** In a lidded jar, combine the marinara sauce, honey, molasses, and salt. Seal tightly, shake vigorously to incorporate, and then chill for up to 7 days.

1   Drain the canned beans. In a small pot, combine the beans and marinara mixture. Bring to a boil, uncovered, then lower to a simmer and cook until the beans soften and are heated through, about 5 minutes. Remove from the heat and cover to keep warm.

2   Serve directly from the pot. Store leftovers in an airtight container, chilled, for up to 4 days.

# BRITISH BAKED BEANS

**PREP:** 2 minutes
**COOK:** 7 minutes
**YIELD:** 4 to 6 servings

⅔ cup marinara sauce (see page 151)

2 tablespoons honey

2 teaspoons molasses

½ teaspoon kosher salt

Two 15-ounce cans great Northern beans or other white beans

# ZESTY "PRALINE" BACON

**PREP:** 7 minutes

**COOK:** 8 to 10 minutes

**YIELD:** 4 servings

---

¼ cup honey

2 teaspoons finely grated lemon zest, plus ½ teaspoon freshly squeezed lemon juice

1 teaspoon Sriracha

¾ cup whole pecans

16 slices nitrate-free bacon (see Note, page 71)

While setting up glamping tents at the Voodoo festival in New Orleans, I discovered Elizabeth's, a sinful brunch spot in the Bywater. It was there that I had my unforgettable first taste of "praline bacon," a pecan-bacon brittle. Though this recipe was inspired by Elizabeth's indulgent dish, you can feel good about eating my lightened-up version for breakfast *every* morning. I swap honey for the sugar, dial down the amount of sweetener, and leave out the butter altogether. Repurpose leftovers as bacon bits in coal-baked potatoes (see page 123).

---

**PREP** In a small jar, combine the honey, lemon zest, lemon juice, and Sriracha. Seal tightly, shake to incorporate, and then store, chilled, for up to 2 weeks. Let come to ambient temperature before assembling the dish.

Preheat the oven to 350°F. Spread the pecans on a rimmed baking sheet. Bake for 5 to 7 minutes, until you smell their aroma; watch closely, as they burn easily. Remove from the oven and let cool. Transfer to a cutting board and mince. Store in an airtight container in a cool, dark place for up to 4 weeks.

1   Line a plate or baking sheet with paper towels.

2   Put 4 slices of the bacon in a cold 12-inch cast-iron skillet or frying pan and set over medium heat. Cook until the bacon is brown and crispy, about 8 minutes total, flipping with tongs every 2 minutes. (Cooking time will vary depending on the thickness of your bacon; the key is to keep a close eye on it.) Transfer the bacon to the prepared plate to let the paper towel absorb the excess grease. Pour the bacon fat from the skillet into a small mason jar, leaving a film on the pan. Add another 4 slices bacon and cook; since the pan is already at heat, the bacon will be more prone to burning, so watch carefully. Transfer to the plate, pour the bacon fat into the same jar, and repeat an additional two times. (When you have cooked the last batch, cool, seal, and chill the bacon fat for up to 6 months to use for frying eggs or roasting potatoes.)

3   While the bacon is still warm, remove the paper towel from beneath the slices. Stir the honey-lemon-Sriracha mixture to reincorporate, then use a spoon to drizzle over both sides of the bacon. Generously scatter the pecans over the bacon.

4   Serve warm. Store leftovers in an airtight container, chilled, for up to 5 days.

# SKILLET BISCUITS WITH EVERYTHING SPICE

PREP: 15 minutes
COOK: 28 minutes
YIELD: 24 biscuits

---

3¼ cups unbleached all-purpose flour

2 tablespoons sugar

2 tablespoons aluminum-free baking powder

1½ teaspoons fine salt

½ cup unsalted butter, ice cold, plus 1½ tablespoons

1 recipe Everything Spice (page 65)

1⅓ cups buttermilk

1 egg

Note: If you are cooking the biscuits at home, bake them on a parchment paper-lined baking sheet in a 425°F oven for 12 minutes. Transfer to a wire rack to cool.

When I was training as a backcountry guide, I awoke one morning before sunrise to banging and shuffling sounds— I was certain it was a bear. I peeked out from my tent, ready to brace myself but instead found our leader preparing biscuits from scratch, hoping to have them ready before the rest of us were up. Skillet biscuits are a cross between an oven-baked biscuit and an English muffin: thin, hearty, flaky, and rich. The homemade Everything Spice, inspired by the everything bagel, takes them to another level. If you don't like Everything Spice, feel free to add your favorite fresh herbs or spices to the dough. It's best to prepare the dough at home and freeze the rounds until ready to pack for camp. Skillet biscuits tend to be doughy when piping hot, but dry out once cold. For a happy medium, allow biscuits to cool slightly and then serve warm; they are a great complement to any meal. No matter what you do, don't forget to have butter on hand.

---

**PREP** In a large bowl, combine the flour, sugar, baking powder, and salt and stir with a fork to mix.

Working over the bowl, use a paring knife to cut the ½ cup ice-cold butter into slivers, letting them drop into the flour mixture. Use your fingers to massage the butter into the flour mixture until it resembles coarse sand. Stir in the Everything Spice.

In a medium bowl, whisk together the buttermilk and egg.

Make a well in the flour mixture. Pour in the buttermilk mixture and use a spatula to fold together until thoroughly combined. The dough will be sticky.

Without kneading, use your hands to form the dough into a ball. (It's helpful to flour your hands to prevent them from sticking to the dough.) Transfer to a heavily floured, clean surface, like a cutting board or baking sheet. With the palms of your hands, flatten the dough into a rough 11 by 13-inch rectangle about 1 inch thick. Using a narrow-mouth mason jar, cup, or 2½- to 3-inch cookie cutter, cut circles from the dough. (You can flour the mouth of your jar or cutter if it gets sticky.) Gather the dough scraps together, flatten the dough again, and cut out more circles. You should have about 24 biscuits.

continued

Wrap each biscuit individually with plastic wrap and store in an airtight container or ziplock bag. Chill for up to 1 day or freeze for up to 6 months. If packing frozen biscuits in your cooler, they will begin to defrost and hold for up to 3 days, assuming the cooler is kept very cold.

1   Defrost the biscuits a day before baking. You want them to be very cold when you're ready to cook; this is essential for getting that flaky texture.

2   In a 12-inch cast-iron skillet with a lid over medium heat, melt ½ tablespoon of the remaining butter, allowing it to spread evenly. Once the butter begins to foam (before it browns!), add 8 to 10 biscuits directly from the cooler.

3   Cover the skillet and cook until the biscuits are crispy and brown on the bottom, about 8 minutes. If some biscuits are cooking faster than others, use a spatula to shift them around in the pan—the biscuits in the middle will cook the fastest. Flip the biscuits and cook until the other side is crispy and brown, about 5 minutes more. Remove the pan from the heat and let the biscuits continue to bake in the pan, covered, until ready to serve. To test if the biscuits are fully baked, rip off a small piece and squeeze it; if it is a dough-like consistency, continue cooking the biscuits for 3 to 5 minutes. Repeat this process with the remaining biscuits, adding another ½ tablespoon butter before cooking.

4   Serve warm, directly from pan. Store leftovers in an airtight container at ambient temperature for up to 5 days.

This classic spice mix is redefined by replacing dried onion flakes and garlic powder with fresh ingredients fried in butter. There is no substitute for the caramelized nibs of onion and garlic strewn amid the seeds and coarse sea salt. I recommend preparing this at home, and doubling the recipe if you want to stock your pantry.

# EVERYTHING SPICE

PREP: 5 minutes
COOK: 12 minutes
YIELD: ⅓ cup

1 tablespoon unsalted butter, plus 1 teaspoon

1½ tablespoons minced onion

1½ tablespoons minced garlic

1½ tablespoons sesame seeds

1 tablespoon caraway seeds

2 teaspoons poppy seeds

¾ teaspoon coarse sea salt (preferably sel gris)

1   Line a plate with a paper towel.

2   In a small pan over medium-low heat, melt the 1 table-spoon butter. Once the butter begins to foam (before it browns!), add the onion and cook, stirring occasionally, until brown and crisp, 5 to 7 minutes. Transfer the onion to the prepared plate.

3   Add the 1 teaspoon butter to the pan and let melt. Once the butter begins to foam (before it browns!), add the garlic and cook, stirring frequently, for 3 to 5 minutes, watching carefully so that the garlic doesn't burn. Transfer to the plate with the onion.

4   In a small bowl, combine the sesame seeds, caraway seeds, poppy seeds, and salt. Add the onion and garlic to the seed mixture, stir together with a fork, and set aside until cool.

5   Store in a lidded jar or airtight container in a cool, dark place for up to 3 days, or chill for up to 2 weeks.

# SKILLET HOME FRIES WITH ZESTY ZA'ATAR

PREP: About 10 minutes

COOK: About 20 minutes

YIELD: 4 to 6 servings

---

3 large russet potatoes

½ cup diced yellow onion

1 teaspoon grated garlic

¼ cup unsalted butter, plus ¼ cup as needed

½ teaspoon kosher salt

2 tablespoons Zesty Za'atar (see page 33) or store-bought za'atar seasoning

Home fries are the crowning glory of any breakfast plate, but it's often hard to get a crispy, browned shell and soft, tender inside. This recipe is the result of a dedicated quest to nail that balance. Russet potatoes work best for this dish because their high starch content yields a crusty exterior. It's important to use a 12-inch skillet so the potatoes don't overcrowd and get mushy when cooking. The Zesty Za'atar adds crunchy sesame seeds and a shower of herbs and lemon zest to brighten this notoriously buttery dish. Pair with fried eggs and Zesty "Praline" Bacon (page 60).

---

**PREP** Scrub the potatoes (do not peel), cut into ½-inch cubes, transfer to a ziplock bag, and then chill for up to 24 hours. They may brown a little, but it won't affect the flavor of your dish.

Combine the onion and garlic in another ziplock bag and then chill for up to 7 days.

1   Put the ¼ cup butter in a 12-inch cast-iron skillet or large sauté pan and place over medium heat. (It's important to add the butter when the pan is cold, so it creates a nonstick seal as it heats.) When the butter begins to foam (before it browns!), add the potatoes and salt. Use a spatula to toss the potatoes with the butter and then spread them into an even layer in the pan. Cover the pan and cook undisturbed for 10 minutes.

2   Uncover the pan and toss the potatoes again, letting them settle into an even layer. Cook, uncovered, for 5 minutes. If the potatoes start to look dry and stick to the pan, move them to one side and add 1 tablespoon butter to the cleared side of the pan. Let the butter melt and then toss with the potatoes, spreading again into an even layer, and continue cooking. You can repeat this process with up to 3 tablespoons butter as needed.

3   Add the onion-garlic mixture to the potatoes, toss, and spread into an even layer. Cover the pan and cook for 5 minutes more. Uncover the pan, add the za'atar, and toss to combine. If the home fries still aren't crispy, cook for another 5 minutes; otherwise, remove from the heat. Toss once again, scraping the crispy bits from the bottom of the pan.

4   Serve warm directly from the pan. Store leftovers in an airtight container, chilled, for up to 5 days.

*Frittata* is a code word for making leftover bits and pieces taste *really* good at the end of your camping trip. This version is particularly irresistible, fusing meaty shiitakes and sausages with melted cheese and a bright herbal finish. Another favorite combination is sun-dried tomatoes, goat cheese, and pesto. Just remember for every dozen eggs to add ½ cup milk, which is crucial for a fluffy frittata.

**PREP** In a 10-inch sauté pan over medium-low heat, melt 1 tablespoon of the butter. Once the butter begins to foam (before it browns!), add the sausage and cook until well-done, 10 to 15 minutes. Transfer to a plate to cool and then cut into bite-size pieces.

In the same pan, melt 2 tablespoons butter, scraping the bottom of the pan to loosen any sausage bits. Add the mushrooms and garlic and sauté until the mushrooms are tender, about 5 minutes. If the mushrooms start to look dry halfway through cooking, add 1 tablespoon butter. Add the cooked sausage and the thyme and stir to combine. Remove from the heat, let cool, transfer to an airtight container or ziplock bag, and then chill for up to 4 days.

In a large lidded jar, combine the eggs, milk, salt, and pepper. Seal tightly, shake vigorously, about 10 seconds, until incorporated, and then chill for up to 24 hours.

1   In a 10-inch high-sided sauté or cast-iron pan with a lid over high heat, melt the remaining 2 tablespoons butter. Once the butter begins to foam (before it browns!), add the sausage-mushroom mixture and spread into an even layer. Pour the egg mixture over the sausage and mushrooms and evenly sprinkle with the cheese.

2   Turn the heat to low, cover the pan, and cook until the frittata has set (a knife inserted into the center comes out clean), about 20 minutes. Cut into wedges.

3   Serve warm directly from the pan. Store leftovers in an airtight container, chilled, for up to 4 days.

# SHIITAKE, SAUSAGE, AND CHEDDAR FRITTATA

PREP: 10 minutes
COOK: 35 minutes
YIELD: 6 servings

6 tablespoons unsalted butter

7 small breakfast sausage links (see Note)

2 cups shiitake mushrooms, stemmed and sliced

3 garlic cloves, minced

5 thyme sprigs, leaves stripped

12 eggs

½ cup milk

½ teaspoon kosher salt

20 turns of the pepper mill

1 cup shredded cheddar cheese

Note: I use sausage links that are about 3½ inches long; if you substitute other sizes or patties, the yield should be about 8 ounces.

# BIRD IN A NEST WITH HONEYED AVO

PREP: 5 minutes
COOK: 10 minutes
YIELD: 2 servings

2 slices bread

2 tablespoons unsalted butter

2 eggs

1 avocado

1 teaspoon honey

1 teaspoon red pepper flakes (optional)

Kosher salt and freshly ground black pepper

Bird in a Nest (also known as Toad in the Hole or Spit in the Eye) rallies my inner child, hands waving in the air and squealing, "eggs and toast!" I would always beg for the most over-easy egg so I could dunk my cutout circle of toast into a sunny pool of yolk (which became a brighter yellow after my mom introduced chickens to our backyard). This classic egg dish is one of the easiest to make at camp while still feeling special and hearty. Fresh slices of avocado and a drizzle of honey dress it up just a bit. I find that rustic sourdough or whole-grain bread stands up best to a runny egg. The easiest way to cut circles in your bread is with a narrow-mouth jar, cup, or cookie cutter 2½ to 3 inches in diameter. Serve this alongside British Baked Beans (page 59).

1   Press the mouth of a narrow-mouth jar, cup, or cookie cutter into the center of each slice of bread, cutting out a hole.

2   In a 10-inch cast-iron skillet or sauté pan over medium heat, melt 1 tablespoon of the butter. When the butter begins to foam (before it browns!), add a bread slice and cutout circle in the pan.

3   Crack an egg into the bread hole. Cook, uncovered, until the underside of the bread is golden brown and the egg is set, 1 to 2 minutes. Using a spatula, flip the bread and egg and repeat on the other side. When the egg and toast (including the cut-out) are cooked to the desired consistency, transfer to a camper's plate. Repeat with the remaining bread slice, butter, and egg.

4   Halve the avocado and remove the pit. Slice the avocado halves in their shell, and scoop out with a fork or spoon, fanning the slices over the surface of the egg and toast. Drizzle the honey evenly over the avocado and sprinkle with the red pepper flakes (if using) and salt and pepper.

5   Serve immediately. Leftovers won't keep well, so eat up!

On summer holidays in the Dolomites, my mother had a trick for keeping us moving on the trail: Italian chocolate-bar sandwiches. We would eat half a sandwich before setting off and the other half at the end of the trail, which was always motivation to finish the hike in a timely manner! I used this childhood snack as inspiration when I was on *Food Network Star*. I already trusted in the marriage of chocolate and bread, so I added the saltiness of bacon and the creaminess of burrata. Bobby Flay raved, "Give me bacon, chocolate, and cream and I'll go anywhere with you." So if you're trying to lure friends or family to spend a night outside, drop a few hints about this breakfast sandwich, which is camp- and kid-friendly, relying on a ready-made chocolate-hazelnut spread like the Italian favorite, Nutella.

# CHOCOLATE, BACON, AND BURRATA BREAKFAST SANDWICH

PREP: 10 minutes
COOK: 20 minutes
YIELD: 4 servings

---

**Eight ½-inch-thick slices sourdough bread**

**8 slices sliced, nitrate-free bacon (see Note)**

**½ cup chocolate-hazelnut spread**

**8 ounces fresh burrata or mozzarella, cut into ¼-inch slices**

1   Line a plate with a paper towel. Lay the bread slices on a clean work surface.

2   Put half the bacon in a cold 12-inch cast-iron skillet or frying pan and set over medium heat. Cook until the bacon is brown and crispy, about 8 minutes total, flipping with tongs every 2 minutes. (Cooking time will vary depending on the thickness of your bacon; the key is to keep a close eye on it.) Transfer the bacon to the prepared plate to let the paper towel absorb the excess grease. Pour the bacon fat from the skillet into a small mason jar, leaving a film on the pan. Add the remaining bacon and cook; because the pan is already at heat, the bacon will be more prone to burning, so watch carefully. Transfer to the plate. (When you have cooked the last batch, cool, seal, and chill the bacon fat for up to 6 months to use for frying eggs or roasting potatoes.) Do not rinse the pan.

3   Smear the chocolate-hazelnut spread on 4 slices of the bread, then top each with 2 slices of the bacon, followed by 2 slices of the burrata. Top with the remaining bread slices.

4   Reheat the skillet over medium heat. Place two sandwiches in the skillet at a time, flattening gently with a spatula. Cook until the bottoms brown and the burrata begins to melt, 3 to 5 minutes. Flip the sandwiches and cook, uncovered, until the other side browns, 2 to 3 minutes more. Remove from the pan and cut in half.

5   Serve immediately; leftovers don't keep well.

Note: For a leaner bacon that renders less fat (and leaves you with less mess), choose Canadian or cottage bacon instead of traditional American bacon. Bring a 4-ounce mason jar for storing excess bacon fat.

breakfast

# TIRAMISU FRENCH TOAST WITH STRAWBERRIES

PREP: 10 minutes
COOK: 30 to 45 minutes
YIELD: 4 servings

---

½ cup mascarpone

2 tablespoons strong brewed coffee

1 teaspoon honey

2 pinches grated nutmeg

1 cup milk

2 eggs

1 teaspoon vanilla extract

1 pinch kosher salt

1 baguette, sliced into 1-inch-thick rounds

2 to 3 tablespoons unsalted butter or coconut oil

1 tablespoon unsweetened Dutch-processed cocoa powder

½ cup sliced fresh strawberries

This is an Italian twist on a French dish originally designed to make use of *pain perdu*, or stale bread. For this recipe I use a baguette, which when sliced into rounds and sealed in a ziplock bag is space-saving and holds its shape; it's also the best bread for absorbing the egg batter. Mascarpone, a signature ingredient in tiramisu, is a rich, creamy, spreadable cheese; bring extra for slathering on toasted bread with a drizzle of honey. Surplus baguette slices can be saved for pairing with dips and cheese at happy hour.

---

**PREP** In a food processor or in a bowl with a whisk, combine the mascarpone, coffee, honey, and 1 pinch of the nutmeg and process or beat until smooth. Transfer to an airtight container, seal, and then chill for up to 1 week.

In a lidded jar, combine the milk, eggs, vanilla, salt, and remaining 1 pinch nutmeg. Seal the jar tightly, shake vigorously until the custard is yellow and the yolks are incorporated, 10 seconds, and then chill for up to 24 hours.

1 Place the baguette slices on a rimmed baking sheet and pour the egg custard over them. Use tongs to flip the slices and slather both sides with the custard. Let stand for 5 minutes to absorb the custard. Gently squeeze the slices with the tongs and flip them again to allow the bread to absorb more of the custard. Let stand for another 5 minutes.

2 In a 12-inch cast-iron skillet or large sauté pan over low heat, melt 1 tablespoon of the butter. Once the butter begins to foam (before it browns!), add as many baguette slices as can fit in a single layer and pour any remaining custard over the top. Cover the pan and cook until crispy and golden brown, 10 to 12 minutes. Flip the slices with tongs or a spatula and cook, uncovered, until the other side is crispy and golden brown, about 5 minutes more. Repeat with the remaining baguette slices, melting 1 tablespoon butter in the pan between batches.

3 Serve warm directly from the pan as you finish each batch, or transfer to a plate and cover with aluminum foil to keep warm. Place three slices of French toast on each camper's plate and top with a generous dollop of the mascarpone, which will melt like syrup. Using a fine-mesh strainer, generously dust each serving with cocoa powder and scatter the strawberries over the top. Tell your fellow campers to eat up; leftovers don't keep well.

# SANDWICHES AND SALADS

In this section, you'll find a sandwich guide with hearty, flavor-packed pairings and picnic salads with easy assembly. Double or triple your favorite salads to serve as sides for dinner.

# no-sweat sandwich guide

Use this guide to create the sandwich of your dreams, swapping breads and spreads as you wish. If you don't have time to make the spread, you can nearly always find a substitute at the store.

BREAD ⟶

Sourdough

Rye bread

Bagel

Italian roll

Baguette

Sandwich bread

Pita

Tortilla

Mamma's Famous Chocolate Chip–Banana Bread (page 49)

## HERE ARE SOME FAVORITES:

**BANANA JAM**

mamma's famous chocolate chip–banana bread
+ strawberry jam
+ banana, thinly sliced

**PITA POCKET**

pita
+ smoky baba ghanoush
+ carrots and cucumbers, thinly sliced
+ parsley leaves
+ zesty za'atar

**HAPPY WRAP**

tortilla
+ guacamole in its shell
+ smoked turkey
+ pepper jack cheese
+ sprouts
+ roasted corn salsa

**THE PIGGERY**

sourdough
+ whole-grain honey mustard
+ deli ham
+ cheddar cheese
+ watercress or sprouts
+ sauerkraut or red pepper–fennel kraut

**WILD ALASKAN**

rye bread
+ smoked salmon spread
+ radish, thinly sliced
+ cucumber, thinly sliced
+ quick pickled red onions

**VIETNAMESE STYLE**

baguette
+ vietnamese peanut sauce
+ marinated tofu
+ quick pickles
+ sriracha
+ cilantro leaves

## SPREAD IT →

Easy Italian Mayonnaise
(page 32)

Whole-Grain Honey Mustard
(see page 31)

Smoked Salmon Spread
(page 37)

Basil–Sunflower Seed Pesto
(see page 80)

Pan con Tomate (page 105)

Fruit preserves or jam

Mamma's Salsa Verde
(see page 167)

Vietnamese Peanut Sauce
(see page 149)

Smoky Baba Ghanoush
(page 106)

Classic Creamy Hummus
(page 34)

Guacamole in Its Shell
(page 103)

## STUFF IT →

Hard-boiled egg, thinly sliced

Deli ham or turkey

Salami

Jamón serrano or prosciutto

Zesty "Praline" Bacon
(page 60)

Fire-Licked Skirt Steak
(see page 167)

Crispy Lemon-Thyme Skillet
Chicken (see page 160)

Marinated tofu

Cheddar, pepper Jack,
manchego, or Brie cheese

Radish, thinly sliced

Cucumber, thinly sliced

Watercress, arugula, or
sprouts

Tomato, thinly sliced, or
sun-dried tomatoes

Apple, thinly sliced

Banana, thinly sliced

Anytime Dill and Beet Salad
(page 84)

Raw Kale Caesar Salad
(page 82)

Crushed potato chips

Grilled Eggplant and Zucchini
with Zesty Za'atar (page 119)

Lemon and Parsley Potato
Salad with Honey Mustard
Dressing (page 87)

## SPICE IT

Smoked paprika

Red Pepper–Fennel Kraut
(page 118) or sauerkraut

Quick Pickles (page 38)

Zesty Za'atar (see page 33)

Roasted Corn Salsa
(page 107)

Hot sauce or Sriracha

Cilantro leaves

My half-sister, Rony, was Australian born and raised. Though our visits together are few and far between, our sisterhood is kindred. One summer, Rony and her husband, Simon, worked for room and board at Silver Queen Farm, twenty minutes north of my home in Ithaca, New York. Suddenly, my life was filled with Australian quips, like "cherry toms," and an endless supply of summer squash. Our favorite creation was shaving the squash with a vegetable peeler to create flat, gluten-free noodles—similar to pappardelle pasta—a blank canvas for dressing them up. You'll need a colander to let the noodles drain. This variation was a hit at more than one picnic that summer. Save extra pesto for spooning over a frittata or scrambled eggs, or spreading on a sandwich (see page 76).

1   Shave each summer squash into noodles by holding it firmly at one end and drawing a vegetable peeler up and down while rotating the squash, until you've peeled as much as possible. (Sometimes it's hard to peel the cores; you can save them for snacking, dunking in hummus, or adding to a stir-fry.)

2   Place the squash noodles in a colander and toss with the salt. Let the squash sit for 15 to 30 minutes to allow excess moisture to drain. Rinse the squash and pat dry with paper towel or a clean tea towel. Transfer the squash noodles to a serving bowl; toss with the pesto, olive oil, and cherry toms; and season with pepper.

3   Serve immediately. Set out the Parmesan wedge with a Microplane so campers can grate cheese directly onto their dish.

# SUMMER SQUASH "PAPPAR-DELLE" WITH BASIL–SUNFLOWER SEED PESTO

PREP: 12 minutes
COOK: None
YIELD: 4 servings

2 medium summer squash

2 tablespoons kosher salt

½ cup Basil–Sunflower Seed Pesto (page 80)

2 tablespoons olive oil

⅔ cup halved cherry tomatoes

Freshly ground black pepper

Parmesan wedge for garnishing (optional)

# BASIL–SUNFLOWER SEED PESTO

PREP: 5 minutes
COOK: None
YIELD: 1⅓ cups

---

4 cups packed fresh basil leaves

¾ cup olive oil

1 tablespoon toasted sunflower seeds

2 teaspoons freshly squeezed lemon juice

1 small garlic clove, peeled

½ cup grated Pecorino Romano cheese

½ cup grated Parmesan cheese

Kosher salt (optional)

Pesto is synonymous with basil and pine nuts, though a closer look at its origin from the word *pestare*—"to pound or crush"—suggests it can be made with other greens, nuts, and seeds. I first experimented with pesto when I lived in Ecuador, where pine nuts cost a fortune. My favorite variation was with sunflower seeds, which added an earthy, nutty flavor. This recipe preserves the basil's vibrant green, with added brightness from lemon juice. It is best made at home, giving you leeway to play by swapping basil with parsley, cilantro, kale, arugula, or spinach. Don't add salt until you've tasted the pesto—the cheese might just do the trick! If you're vegan, replace the cheese with ¼ cup nutritional yeast.

---

1   In a colander, gently rinse the basil with cold water. Shake the colander over the sink to remove excess water, allowing a few droplets to cling to the leaves. Set aside.

2   In a blender or food processor, combine ½ cup of the olive oil, the sunflower seeds, lemon juice, and garlic and pulse a few times. Scrape down the sides of the blender or processor bowl, add the basil, pecorino, Parmesan, and remaining ¼ cup olive oil. Pulse until the mixture is smooth and bright green. Taste and season with salt, if needed.

3   Store in an airtight container, chilled, for up to 4 days, or freeze in an ice-cube tray, transferring the cubes to a ziplock bag once frozen. Defrost before using.

# RAW KALE CAESAR SALAD

PREP: About 10 minutes
COOK: None
YIELD: 6 servings

---

1 large bunch kale, any variety

3 anchovy fillets, rinsed and patted dry

3 tablespoons grated Parmesan cheese, plus Parmesan wedge for garnishing (optional)

2 tablespoons freshly squeezed lemon juice, or as needed

1 tablespoon Dijon mustard

1 egg yolk

2 peeled garlic cloves, or as needed

10 turns of the pepper mill

Kosher salt

⅓ cup olive oil, or as needed

Kale is my favorite camping green. It's nutrient dense, stands up to temperature extremes, and can handle being jostled, whereas lettuces and spinach wilt and bruise easily. Raw kale salads are a great way to add fresh vegetables to your camping menu. Massaging the raw kale breaks down the hearty fibers, making it easier to chew and digest. Toppings like toasted nuts, dried cranberries, avocado slices, bacon bits, Not So Devilish Eggs (page 108), leftover Skillet Home Fries with Zesty Za'atar (page 66), or grilled chicken would be more than welcome on this salad. For a creamier dish, double the dressing.

---

**PREP** Wash the kale and pat it dry. Strip the leaves from the stems and slice the leaves into bite-size pieces; compost the stems. Store in an airtight container or ziplock bag, chilled, for up to 5 days.

In a blender, combine the anchovies, grated Parmesan, lemon juice, mustard, egg yolk, garlic, pepper, and ½ teaspoon salt and pulse until a paste forms. With the blender running, pour in the olive oil in a *very thin, very slow*, steady stream and continue to blend until the dressing is smooth and thick. Taste and add more lemon juice, garlic, olive oil, or salt as needed. Transfer to an airtight container and chill for up to 3 days.

1   Place the kale in a serving bowl (unless serving directly from the container), and pour in half of the dressing. Use your hands to massage the dressing into the kale, scrunching and squeezing until the kale reduces in volume by about half and absorbs the dressing, about 30 seconds. Toss with the remaining dressing, or let campers spoon it over their serving.

2   Serve immediately. Set out the Parmesan wedge with a Microplane so campers can grate cheese directly onto their salad.

*Lentilles du Puy* cook twice as fast as their red, yellow, and brown cousins. It's no wonder the "caviar of lentils" held a special place in my mother's kitchen, where she fed a constant rotation of family and friends. These protein-packed beads hold their shape as they swell with water or stock, finishing with a nutty, al dente flavor. Don't confuse this variety with the more common green lentil; *lentilles du Puy* are available in some grocery stores, specialty shops, and online. Substitute with any brown or green lentils and follow the cooking instructions on the bag; they won't hold their shape as well but you'll still have a flavorful meal. This dish is best prepared a day in advance and served cold; the onions lose their bite the longer they marinate with the dressing. Double up on the dressing for an extra-flavorful, creamy dish, and serve with Charred Bread (page 102) to mop up your plate.

---

**PREP** To make the dressing: In a lidded jar, combine the olive oil, vinegar, yogurt, lemon zest, lemon juice, mustard, salt, and pepper. Seal the jar tightly, shake vigorously until incorporated, and then chill for up to 1 week.

In a pot over high heat, combine 4 cups water and the lentils. Bring to a boil, then lower to a simmer, cover, and cook until the lentils are tender but still al dente, about 20 minutes. Drain the lentils and rinse with cold water. Transfer to an airtight container and then chill for up to 3 days.

Combine the onion and parsley in an airtight container and then chill for up to 3 days.

1   Transfer the lentils to a serving bowl. Pour in the dressing; add the onion and parsley, 1¼ cups of the feta, and the prunes (if using); and toss together until everything is evenly coated. Sprinkle the remaining ¼ cup feta over the top.

2   Serve cold. Store leftovers in an airtight container, chilled, for up to 5 days.

# LEMONY FRENCH LENTIL SALAD WITH FETA

PREP: 15 minutes
COOK: 25 minutes
YIELD: 6 to 8 servings

**DRESSING**

---

¼ cup olive oil

2 tablespoons apple cider vinegar

1 tablespoon plain Greek yogurt

Finely grated zest of 1 lemon, plus 1 tablespoon freshly squeezed lemon juice

2 teaspoons Dijon mustard

1 teaspoon kosher salt

20 turns of the pepper mill

2 cups French green (Puy) lentils, checked for stones and rinsed

½ cup minced red onion

1 cup finely chopped fresh parsley

1½ cups crumbled feta

1 cup finely chopped prunes (optional)

# ANYTIME DILL AND BEET SALAD

PREP: 10 minutes

COOK: 20 to 30 minutes

YIELD: 4 servings

---

2 tablespoons mayonnaise
(see page 32)

2 tablespoons apple cider vinegar

1 tablespoon olive oil

1 teaspoon kosher salt

Freshly ground black pepper

8 medium beets

1½ cups loosely packed dill fronds

One winter I was ankle-deep in snow, grilling a whole chicken in my backyard, trying to drum up a side dish. I was uninspired by the beets that had been in my vegetable drawer for months, but then a thought dawned on me. If I serve them cold, tossed with fresh herbs and a bright dressing, they will feel like a salad and less like the dead of winter! This is a refreshing and delicious dish for any season.

---

**PREP** In a lidded jar, combine the mayonnaise, vinegar, olive oil, and salt and season with pepper. Seal the jar tightly, shake vigorously until incorporated, and then chill for up to 1 week.

Scrub the beets and slice off the tip and stems. (Leave the skins on to help the beets retain their color and nutrients when you boil them.) Place the beets in a large pot and add enough cold water to cover. Bring to a boil, then lower to a simmer, cover, and cook until a fork easily pierces the center of the thickest beet, 20 to 30 minutes. Drain the beets and rinse with cold water. Once cool, peel the skin from the beets with your hands (it should slide off fairly easily) and compost it. Halve the beets, then cut into very thin slices, about ⅛ inch thick. Store in an airtight container or ziplock bag, chilled, for up to 3 days.

1   Mince the dill.

2   Transfer the beets to a serving bowl (unless serving directly from the container). Pour the dressing over the beets, add the dill, and toss together until everything is evenly coated.

3   Serve cold. Store leftovers in an airtight container, chilled, for up to 1 week.

Potatoes are virtually indestructible and store well, making them the perfect culinary companion for any outdoor adventure. When I lived in Ecuador—home to more than 2,000 native varieties of potato—they were a staple on weekend climbing trips. I used locally available ingredients to create this creamy, bright variation of a classic American picnic salad. Don't bypass the capers, which add a bright burst; if you're using capers packed in salt, rinse them first. It's important to assemble this dish when the potatoes are warm and can absorb the dressing, but the final dish improves after marinating while chilled. If desired, prepare the night before and serve cold for lunch the next day.

**PREP** To make the dressing: In a lidded jar, combine the mustard, olive oil, lemon juice, honey, salt, and pepper. Seal tightly and shake vigorously to combine. For a creamier dressing, whiz in a blender. Store in an airtight container, chilled, for up to 2 weeks.

Combine the parsley, onion, celery (if using), raisins, and capers in an airtight container or ziplock bag and then chill for up to 3 days.

1   Quarter the potatoes.

2   In a large pot, combine the potatoes with enough cold water to cover and bring to a boil, Lower the heat to a gentle simmer and cook until the potatoes are fork-tender, about 15 minutes. Drain the potatoes and return to the pot.

3   Pour the dressing over the warm potatoes, add the parsley mixture, and toss together until everything is evenly coated.

4   Serve warm directly from the pot. Store leftovers in an airtight container, chilled, for up to 5 days.

# LEMON AND PARSLEY POTATO SALAD WITH HONEY MUSTARD DRESSING

PREP: 20 minutes
COOK: 15 minutes
YIELD: 6 to 8 servings

## HONEY MUSTARD DRESSING

¼ cup Dijon mustard

¼ cup olive oil

3 tablespoons freshly squeezed lemon juice

2 tablespoons honey (preferably local)

¼ teaspoon kosher salt

8 grinds of the pepper mill

2 cups finely chopped fresh parsley

1 cup diced red onion

1 cup diced celery (optional)

1 cup raisins

3 tablespoons capers

8 to 10 medium red potatoes

# CAROL'S FAVORITE PASTA SALAD WITH TOMATOES, BASIL, AND MOZZARELLA

PREP: 15 minutes
COOK: 15 minutes
YIELD: 4 to 6 servings

6 plum tomatoes

8 ounces mozzarella, diced

2 teaspoons grated garlic

½ cup olive oil

Kosher salt

2⅔ cups penne pasta

10 turns of the pepper mill

1 cup packed fresh basil leaves

Parmesan wedge for garnishing (optional)

Carol, my beloved childhood nanny, spent her life in Jamaica before joining our family in Denver. Although she wasn't prepared for all the snow, my mother desperately needed her help, having her own hands full with me and my twin sister. While I like to think our cuteness had a hand in wooing Carol to stay, it was actually my mother's cooking; and this recipe was Carol's favorite. Five years later, Carol left our family after a fierce battle with breast cancer. My mother continued to make "Carol's pasta" in heaping portions whenever our school teams had a big game because she could prepare it the day before and serve it cold at the field. After a win, we would all say, "Must have been Carol's favorite pasta!" It can be prepared in advance and served as a picnic salad after marinating while chilling. For protein, add leftover Crispy Lemon-Thyme Skillet Chicken (see page 160) or canned seafood. Leftover pasta salad is also delicious pan-fried in olive oil until crispy.

PREP Halve, seed, and dice the tomatoes. (Reserve the seeds and juice for making Pan con Tomate, page 105, if you like.) Transfer to a large airtight container and then chill for up to 4 days.

In an airtight container, gently toss together the mozzarella, garlic, and olive oil and then chill for up to 4 days.

1   Fill a large pot with water and bring to a rolling boil. Stir in just enough salt to make the water as salty as the ocean and then add the pasta. Stir with a spoon, return the water to a boil, and cook the pasta until al dente, about 11 minutes. Drain the pasta and return it to the pot.

2   While the pasta is still hot, add the diced tomatoes and mozzarella mixture, and stir until the cheese melts. Toss with 1 teaspoon salt and the pepper. Use your fingers to tear the basil leaves into small pieces and toss into the pasta.

3   Serve warm or cold. Set out the Parmesan wedge with a Microplane so campers can grate cheese directly onto their dish. Store leftovers in an airtight container, chilled, for up to 5 days.

The yogurt-based dressing here creates a creamier-than-ever slaw, and a touch of mayonnaise offers the slightest nod to its classic origins. Fresh parsley gives a bright, earthy dimension, and the toasted pecans add a buttery crunch. For the creative cook, replace some of the cabbage with other shredded root veggies, like kohlrabi, carrots, and watermelon radishes. The longer salted cabbage sits, the soggier it becomes, so dress the slaw just before serving.

**PREP** Core and quarter the cabbage. Trim the ends from the carrots. Use a food processor or sharp knife to finely slice or shred the cabbage and carrots.

Combine the cabbage, carrots, pecans, and parsley in a ziplock bag and then chill for up to 3 days.

In a lidded jar, combine the yogurt, mayonnaise, lemon juice, shallot, vinegar, mustard, and salt. Seal the jar tightly, shake vigorously until incorporated, and then chill for up to 1 week.

1   In a large bowl, combine the cabbage mixture and dressing and toss together until everything is evenly coated.

2   Serve immediately. Store leftovers in an airtight container, chilled, for up to 5 days.

# CLASSIC CREAMY SLAW WITH PECANS

PREP: 15 minutes
COOK: None
YIELD: 6 to 8 servings

1 small head red or green cabbage

2 medium carrots

1½ cups coarsely chopped toasted pecans

1 bunch parsley, leaves stripped and finely chopped

1 cup plain Greek yogurt

2 tablespoons mayonnaise (see page 32)

2 tablespoons freshly squeezed lemon juice

1 small shallot, minced or grated

2 teaspoons apple cider vinegar

1 teaspoon Dijon mustard

1½ teaspoons kosher salt

# HAPPY
# HOUR

After a full day on the trail,
nothing hits the spot like a
cocktail to cool the sweat or
glühwein to thaw your hands.
Here are a few ways to kick off
happy hour and tide you over
until dinner; you deserve it.

# SCORCHED LEMON-ADE

PREP: 5 minutes
COOK: 3 minutes
YIELD: 6 to 8 servings

8 medium lemons, halved crosswise

2 to 3 tablespoons maple syrup

4 cups cold water

Ice cubes for serving

8 fresh mint leaves

I first discovered this spin on lemonade at a summer cook-out in Maine. Charring the lemons gives them a caramel-sweet, smoky flavor that takes you straight to the campfire. For a British-style pub shandy, mix lemonade with pilsner beer in equal parts. For a hot toddy, substitute hot water and add a generous splash of brandy or bourbon.

1   Fire the grill or campfire to medium-high heat and position the grill grate 4 inches above the coals.

2   Place the lemon halves, cut-sides down, over direct heat. Cook until the flesh is caramel brown, 2 to 3 minutes; a toasted caramel smell will also signal when they are ready. Transfer the lemons to a bowl, container, or clean work surface and let cool.

3   Using a lemon squeezer, squeeze the lemons into a pitcher or other serving vessel. Add 2 tablespoons of the maple syrup, stir with a long-handled spoon to incorporate, taste, and add the remaining 1 tablespoon maple syrup if needed. Add the water and stir until incorporated, about 30 seconds.

4   Serve over ice, garnished with the mint leaves.

In Nicaragua, every cantina serves a similar refreshing infusion, which has almost all the elements of a power-ade. The traditional drink is a heavily sweetened iced tea made with the abundant hibiscus flower. When my husband, Bobby, and I opened our hostel in Matagalpa, La Buena Onda, I wanted to serve a version that would reboot weary backpackers who hadn't yet adjusted to the tropical climate. By adding a pinch of salt and cutting back on the sugar, I created a true energy drink that introduced our guests to local flavors. It's been a staple for me on the trail ever since. This can also be served warm, which enhances the soothing qualities of the cinnamon, making it a perfect nightcap.

1   In a small pot with a lid, bring the water to a boil, then remove from the heat. Add the tea bags, cinnamon sticks, lime juice, honey, and salt and stir together. Cover the pot and let steep for 10 minutes. Remove and compost the tea bags and cinnamon stick.

2   Serve warm in mugs, or let cool and serve over ice. Fill your water bottle for the trail, too! Store in a lidded jar, chilled, for up to 5 days.

# HIBISCUS LIME POWER-ADE

PREP: 5 minutes
COOK: 10 minutes
YIELD: 4 servings

1 quart water

2 hibiscus tea bags or 2 tablespoons loose leaf hibiscus flower

2 cinnamon sticks

¼ cup freshly squeezed lime juice

2 tablespoons honey

⅛ teaspoon fine sea salt

Ice cubes for serving (optional)

# CAMPARI SANGRIA SPRITZ

PREP: 30 minutes

COOK: None

YIELD: 6 to 8 servings

---

**Heaping 2 cups strawberries, thinly sliced**

**4 orange slices, halved**

**One 750-ml bottle dry white wine**

**1 cup Campari**

**2 cups seltzer water**

**Ice cubes for serving**

Don't let your kids confuse this with a Shirley Temple (like I did growing up). This fruity variation on an Italian cocktail spells F-U-N. You can substitute the fruit with Amma's Fruit Salad with Honey, Lime, and Mint (page 58).

---

1 In a large pitcher or other serving vessel, combine the strawberries, orange slices, wine, and Campari. Let infuse for 30 minutes, then stir in the seltzer with a long-handled metal spoon.

2 Serve over ice.

Note: Store leftovers in the same serving vessel or a narrow-mouth jar or pitcher for up to 24 hours. Insert the handle of the spoon into the vessel so the bowl of the spoon rests on the edge of the vessel's mouth, and outside and above the vessel; this will preserve the bubbles in the seltzer.

# NORTH STAR GLÜHWEIN

**PREP:** 5 minutes
**COOK:** 20 minutes
**YIELD:** 6 to 8 servings

5 cups red wine

6 orange slices

2 cinnamon sticks

2 star anise

5 whole cloves

2 tablespoons honey, or to taste

¾ to 1 cup rum (optional)

My twin sister, Dimity, and I discovered glühwein when we were penniless college students in Prague, and it has since become our favorite way to settle in around the campfire after a long day of rock climbing. Choose an inexpensive, fruity red wine (bottled or boxed) and let the mulling spices do their work.

1   In a medium pot, combine the wine, orange slices, cinnamon sticks, star anise, cloves, and honey. Bring to a boil, then lower to a simmer, cover, and cook until the wine is infused, about 15 minutes.

2   Serve warm in mugs, adding additional honey and rum as desired.

My freewheeling childhood friend Annie first taught me how to make this spirited tonic on a girlfriends' retreat in Vermont, and soon after served them at her mountain wedding in Jackson Hole. This cocktail goes hand in hand with jumping off rope-swings into lakes, dancing in meadows, and giggling until your stomach hurts. Turn it up a notch with smoked sea salt. You will need two mason jars.

1   In a small bowl or container, combine the lime zest and salt. Stir to mix and then set aside.

2   In each mason jar, combine half of the lime juice, half of the tequila, 1½ teaspoons agave nectar, and 4 ice cubes. Add enough seltzer to come to within ½ inch of the rim. Seal the jars tightly and shake vigorously until frothy, about 30 seconds. Remove the lids and sprinkle the zest-salt mixture around the rims, letting a few salt crystals fall in.

3   Serve immediately.

# MASON JAR MARGS

PREP: 5 minutes
COOK: None
YIELD: 2 servings

Finely grated zest of 1 lime, plus juice of 2 limes

1 teaspoon coarse sea salt or smoked sea salt

¼ cup silver or gold tequila

1 tablespoon agave nectar

8 ice cubes

About 2 cups seltzer water

This Mary is all about the smoked sea salt rim and charred pepperoncini. If charring the pepperoncini at home in a pan, the capsaicin (the spicy element in hot peppers) will be more concentrated when it's released; so if you're sensitive to spice, it might make you cough when cooking. Open the windows and air out the kitchen before you start. Don't splurge on the vodka; a relatively cheap one will do. Look for a tomato juice that specifies "100% juice" on the label, and doesn't contain any ingredients that are unfamiliar or hard to pronounce.

**PREP** To make the Smoky Mary Mix: In a large lidded jar or airtight container, combine the tomato juice, pepperoncini juice, lemon juice, horseradish, Worcestershire, soy sauce, salt, and pepper. Seal tightly, shake vigorously until combined, about 30 seconds, and then chill for up to 1 month.

1   In a 10-inch pan (I prefer cast iron for even charring) over high heat, warm the sunflower oil. When the oil begins to smoke, add the pepperoncini and, using tongs, rotate until blistered, about 7 minutes. Be careful at first, as the water content in the pepperoncini will splatter.

2   Spread the 2 teaspoons smoked sea salt on a plate or in a bowl. Rub the rim of a mason jar or camp cup with a lemon slice. Turn the rim of the glass in the salt to coat. Place the glass upright on a flat surface. Add about 4 ice cubes, 2 tablespoons vodka, and ½ cup Smoky Mary Mix and stir to combine. Garnish with the same lemon slice and a charred pepperoncino. Repeat to make the remaining cocktails.

3   Serve immediately.

# SMOKY MARYS WITH CHARRED PEPPER-ONCINI

PREP: 15 minutes
COOK: 7 minutes
YIELD: 8 servings

**SMOKY MARY MIX**

4 cups pure tomato juice

½ cup pepperoncini juice (from one 12-ounce jar pepperoncini, preferably Greek or Italian)

Juice of 2½ lemons

3 tablespoons prepared horseradish

4 teaspoons Worcestershire sauce

1 teaspoon soy sauce or tamari sauce

1 teaspoon smoked sea salt

1 teaspoon freshly ground black pepper

2 teaspoons sunflower oil

8 pepperoncini (see Note)

2 teaspoons smoked sea salt

8 lemon slices

Ice cubes for serving

1 cup vodka

Note: You can also grill the pepperoncini 4 inches above medium-high coals, rotating until blistered, about 5 minutes.

# the grazing table

A grazing table can be a light snack, an easy picnic, or a full meal, but it always revolves around simple pairings like cheese and pears. In Italy, they have a saying, *Al contadin non far sapere quanto e' buon il formaggio con le pere,* which translates to "Don't let the farmer know how good cheese and pears are together." The idea being, if you did, he would never sell either to you.

Assemble your spread in a central place that can be accessed from all angles. Don't bother with fancy servingware or pristine picnic blankets; crumbs and blobs of dip will spill, as they should. Cutting boards are helpful for serving cheese and slicing fruit, and you can pile the bread on a kitchen towel or parchment or butcher paper. Many of the dips, spreads, and spice mixes are easily prepared at home, so you can get right to nibbling at camp without worrying about cooking and cleanup.

While there are no hard-and-fast rules, the following guidelines will help you create a balanced spread.

**Bread:** Fresh or charred bread slices (see page 102), pita, or crackers (with gluten-free options)

**Crudités:** Sliced vegetables and fresh fruit

**Sweet:** Hard-Cider Butter (page 129), jams, and jellies

**Savory:** Maple-Rosemary Roasted Almond Mix (page 39), Zesty Za'atar Olive Oil Dip (page 33), Classic Creamy Hummus (page 34), Smoky Baba Ghanoush (page 106), Pan con Tomate (page 105), and Basil–Sunflower Seed Pesto (see page 80)

**Sour:** Quick Pickles (page 38)

**Creamy:** A small selection of cheeses and whipped butter

**Hearty:** Smoked Salmon Spread (page 37), Not So Devilish Eggs (page 108), and charcuterie

# CHARRED BREAD

PREP: 5 minutes

COOK: 8 minutes

YIELD: 8 servings

___

**1 loaf unsliced whole-grain bread with a hard crust (preferably sourdough)**

**¼ cup olive oil**

When I was growing up, the crackle of hands tearing into fresh bread was always part of the racket at the dinner table. My mother would set out a baguette or an Italian country loaf alongside dinner, and we would pass it around, peeling off chunks to dip in olive oil or mop our plates clean. The simple act of sharing a loaf reinforced our connection to each other and our food. When bread is toasted on the grill or campfire, the fire forms a smoky crust on the exposed interior, or "crumb," that's primal in flavor. You can never prepare too much bread, ever. It stretches a meal; and if you're lucky, it will stretch into tomorrow's sandwiches. People always ask how I make this bread, and the answer is incredibly simple.

___

**PREP** Cut the bread into ¾-inch slices and then cut those in half again. Put the bread slices into a large bowl or on a baking sheet, generously drizzle with the olive oil, and toss with your hands to coat. Seal in a ziplock bag and store at ambient temperature for up to 24 hours.

1   Fire the grill or campfire to high heat and position the grill grate about 2 inches above the coals.

2   Using tongs, lay six bread slices at a time over direct heat, charring the slices for 30 to 60 seconds before flipping and repeating on the other side. Shift the slices to indirect heat as needed but don't be afraid of a dark char or slight burn—it's delicious—though you can also scrape the burned bits off with a knife. Repeat with the remaining slices. Transfer the charred bread to a serving bowl, cutting board, or directly onto a sheet of butcher paper on the table.

3   Serve warm or cool. Store leftovers in a ziplock bag at ambient temperature for up to 2 days.

This quick guacamole was my go-to snack as a kid. It's mashed right in the avocado shell with a simple dressing and then scooped straight out with a spoon or hunk of bread—no dishes to clean! This was also my daughter's first morsel of solid food, and continues to be a family favorite at home, on the trail, and on the road. To make this dip for a crowd, mash the ingredients in a large bowl, and save leftovers for spreading on a sandwich (see page 76). To be sure an avocado is ripe, remove the knobby stem; if the fruit is green beneath, it's ready to eat.

**PREP** In a small lidded jar or airtight container, combine the olive oil, balsamic vinegar, and salt. Shake vigorously to incorporate and then store in a cool, dark place for up to 1 month.

1   Line up the avocado halves, flesh-side up.

2   Shake the olive oil–vinegar mixture to reincorporate, and pour 1½ teaspoons into the hollows of the avocado halves where the pit was removed. Sprinkle pepper over the top and garnish with 1 teaspoon of herbs, if desired.

3   Each camper can use their fork to mash everything right in the shell, and scoop up the guacamole with charred bread or tortilla chips. Leftovers don't keep well, so eat up!

# GUACAMOLE IN ITS SHELL

PREP: 5 minutes
COOK: None
YIELD: 6 servings

---

**2 tablespoons olive oil**

**1 tablespoon balsamic vinegar**

**1 tablespoon kosher salt**

**3 ripe avocados, halved and pitted**

**Freshly ground black pepper**

**½ cup fresh parsley or cilantro leaves, minced (optional)**

**Charred Bread (facing page) or tortilla chips for scooping**

My Spanish roommate in Ecuador, Sara, first introduced me to this Catalan dip, one of many dishes she made when she was homesick. Most restaurants in Barcelona and throughout Catalonia serve a more basic version—toasted bread rubbed with a garlic clove and the flesh side of a halved tomato, and then drizzled with olive oil. But to Sara, a mere hint of tomato was not enough—she wanted the bread drenched in tomato sauce. When you try Sara's herbed version, you'll agree. Make this when tomatoes are in season, or with ½ cup strained tomato puree such as Pomi. Serve with an assortment of spreads, cheeses, and cured meats.

---

**PREP** In a small lidded jar or airtight container, combine the olive oil, oregano, garlic, salt, and pepper. Shake vigorously to incorporate and then store in a cool, dark place for up to 1 month.

1   Halve the tomatoes. Using a Microplane, grate the cut side of the tomatoes over a small bowl, collecting the grated flesh and juices. Shake the olive oil mixture to reincorporate, and stir into the tomato juice.

2   Serve in the same bowl, alongside charred bread, either dunking the bread straight in the dip or using a spoon to spread the dip on the bread. Store leftovers in an airtight container, chilled, for up to 1 week.

# PAN CON TOMATE

PREP: 2 minutes
COOK: None
YIELD: 6 servings

---

½ cup olive oil

1 tablespoon dried or minced fresh oregano

½ teaspoon grated garlic

½ teaspoon kosher salt

10 turns of the pepper mill

1 large or 2 medium heirloom or beefsteak tomatoes (see Note)

12 slices Charred Bread (page 102)

Note: Season the leftover tomato skins with olive oil, salt, and pepper and then char on the grill.

# SMOKY BABA GHANOUSH

PREP: 15 minutes

COOK: 30 minutes

YIELD: 4 to 6 servings

---

¼ cup tahini, at room temperature

2 or 3 garlic cloves, grated

2 tablespoons freshly squeezed lemon juice

½ teaspoon kosher salt

1 medium eggplant

2 teaspoons olive oil, plus ¼ cup

1 tablespoon fresh parsley leaves (optional)

¼ teaspoon smoked paprika (optional)

Note: To cook the eggplant on a gas stove-top, place the eggplant directly over a medium-high flame, rotating with tongs, until the exterior is evenly charred on all sides and the eggplant is very soft. If the center is still firm, place the eggplant halves flesh-side down on a baking sheet and bake at 350°F until fully cooked, 15 to 25 minutes.

To cook the eggplant in the oven, preheat the oven to 375°F and line a baking sheet with aluminum foil. Prick the skin of the eggplant with a fork so the entire eggplant is pocked with holes—this will help steam release in the oven. Cut the eggplant in half and place on the baking sheet flesh-side down. Bake until the inside flesh is very soft to the touch, 30 to 45 minutes.

Serve this baba ghanoush with bread, toasted pita, or raw vegetables, or spread it on a sandwich (see page 76). When selecting an eggplant, look for one with taut, shiny, smooth skin. If you would like to cook the eggplant before heading to your campsite, see the Note. If you prefer a smoother, less-rustic baba ghanoush, make the whole recipe at home and puree the cooked eggplant and remaining ingredients in a blender or food processor.

---

PREP In a lidded jar or airtight container, combine the tahini, garlic, lemon juice, and salt; stir to mix thoroughly; and then chill for up to 1 week.

1   Fire the grill or campfire to medium-high heat and position the grill grate 4 inches above the coals.

2   Using tongs, place the eggplant over direct heat. Cook until the bottom is evenly charred, about 5 minutes. Rotate the eggplant and continue to cook until the exterior is evenly charred on all sides and the eggplant is very soft, 15 to 20 minutes total. Let cool slightly.

3   When cool enough to handle, halve the eggplant lengthwise. If the interior is still firm, brush each flesh side with 1 teaspoon of the olive oil, place them flesh-side down on the grill, and cook until mushy and charred, up to 10 minutes more. (You might choose to do this anyway for a smokier flavor.) Once halved, use a spoon to scoop the eggplant flesh into a large bowl; compost the skins. Using a fork, mash the eggplant into a chunky or smooth consistency—your call!

4   Add the tahini mixture to the eggplant and mash together with the fork. Drizzle in the ¼ cup olive oil while mashing and continue to mash until incorporated. Drizzle the remaining 1 teaspoon olive oil over the top.

5   Mince the parsley (if using) and sprinkle over the eggplant.

6   Serve warm or cold, garnished with the paprika (if using). Store leftovers in an airtight container, chilled, for up to 5 days.

Every camp needs a jar of salsa. Or two. Or three. Served with tortilla chips, salsa provides a quick, hearty snack for hungry campers. This roasted corn salsa spiffs up eggs and nachos in a heartbeat. After making this once, you'll probably want to double the next batch and keep extra on hand. Don't bypass roasting the corn—it *makes* the salsa. Spring onions, also called green onions, are often available at the supermarket alongside scallions. They are sweeter and milder than a red or yellow onion but have more bite than scallions (which are best used for garnish). They also add a perfect kick to this salsa without destroying your breath for the rest of the day. You'll be grateful you took the time to toast and crush whole coriander seeds, which add a nutty dimension to the spice's citrus characteristics.

**PREP** In a large bowl, combine the tomatoes, spring onions, olive oil, lemon juice, vinegar, honey, garlic, Sriracha, salt, and coriander seeds and toss together with a spoon. Transfer to an airtight container and then chill for up to 5 days.

1   Fire the grill or campfire to medium-high heat and position the grill grate 2 to 4 inches above the coals.

2   Place the ears of corn over direct heat and, using tongs, rotate every 2 to 3 minutes until the ears are uniformly charred and the kernels bright yellow, 10 to 12 minutes. For a darker char, drizzle olive oil over the corn so it drips onto the coals and the flames jump up to lick the corn.

3   Using a sharp chef's knife, hold an ear of corn at a slant so one end is resting on a clean surface or in the base of a bowl. Slice the kernels off the cob by drawing the knife down from the top end to the bottom. Transfer the kernels to the container with the tomato mixture and stir to incorporate.

4   Serve immediately. Store leftovers in an airtight container, chilled, for up to 5 days.

# ROASTED CORN SALSA

PREP: 15 minutes
COOK: 12 minutes
YIELD: 2½ cups

---

**2 cups seeded and finely diced plum tomatoes**

**½ cup diced spring onions**

**2 tablespoons olive oil, or as needed**

**2 tablespoons lemon or lime juice**

**2 teaspoons apple cider vinegar**

**1 teaspoon honey**

**1 teaspoon grated garlic**

**1 teaspoon Sriracha or 1 jalapeño chile, seeded and minced**

**1 teaspoon kosher salt**

**1 teaspoon toasted coriander seeds, crushed**

**3 ears corn, shucked**

# NOT SO DEVILISH EGGS

PREP: 5 minutes
COOK: 12 minutes
YIELD: 6 to 8 servings

---

12 eggs

¼ cup olive oil

¼ cup Zesty Za'atar (see page 33)

½ teaspoon smoked paprika (optional)

Deviled eggs are sumptuous starters in a domestic setting but can be devilishly tedious when it comes to camping. This is my more angelic version; easy on you, bursting with flavor, and ready to satisfy hunger pangs, pre- or post-hike. Boiling the eggs at home makes them easier to transport to camp. Top a Raw Kale Caesar Salad (page 82) with leftovers.

---

**PREP** Place the eggs in a large pot and add enough cold water to cover. Bring to a boil, then turn off the heat, cover the pot, and let stand for 10 minutes (set a timer). Drain the eggs in a colander and rinse with cold water or soak them in a bowl of ice water until cool to the touch (it's rumored to help the peels come off more easily). Chill the eggs in their shells until ready to peel, up to 1 week.

1   Cut the hard-boiled eggs into ½-inch slices and arrange on a serving plate in a single layer or with the edges overlapping, like dominoes. Drizzle the olive oil over the egg slices and sprinkle with the za'atar. Dust with the smoked paprika, if desired.

2   Serve immediately.

Note: If you want to make a more "true" deviled egg, slice the eggs in half and transfer the yolks to a bowl. Mash with the olive oil and then spoon the yolks back into their halves before topping with the za'atar and paprika.

Typically, there are two choices for campfire popcorn: Jiffy Pop or a foil satchel of kernels that produces a mere handful of popped corn. I wanted a version that would taste better than Jiffy Pop while making enough to stuff my face. The result, modeled after the Jiffy Pop pan, is an easy craft project you can assemble at home before heading to camp. You'll need an 8-inch disposable aluminum pie plate, heavy-duty aluminum foil, and a stapler. The seasoning in this recipe is unique and tantalizing, blending crushed seaweed and cheesy nutritional yeast, which is high in Vitamin B12. The smoked sea salt amplifies the campfire experience, and is easily found online and at some grocery stores.

# CAMPFIRE POPCORN WITH SEA SMOKE

PREP: 5 minutes
COOK: 10 minutes
YIELD: 2 servings

¼ cup popcorn kernels

2 tablespoons vegetable oil

1 tablespoon unsalted butter, melted

5 to 10 sheets roasted seaweed (see Note), crumbled

2 tablespoons nutritional yeast (optional)

½ teaspoon smoked sea salt

**PREP** Fill an 8-inch aluminum pie plate with the popcorn kernels and vegetable oil. Cover the pie plate with a 12-inch sheet of heavy-duty aluminum foil; the foil should not be taut, leave it loose so it can expand to a 3-inch-high tent when the popcorn pops. Staple the edges of the foil to the edges of the pie plate. Wrap tightly in plastic wrap, so the oil doesn't leak, and store in a cool, dark place up to 2 weeks.

1   Prepare your campfire ahead of time so you have hot, glowing red coals at medium-high heat. Remove the pie plate from the plastic wrap.

2   Using long-handled metal tongs, grip as close to the pan's edge as possible and hover it over the hot coals. When the popcorn starts popping, after about 5 minutes, start shaking the pan continuously to prevent the kernels from burning. When the kernels stop popping, 3 to 5 minutes, you're done!

3   Remove the pan from the fire and poke the top of the foil with a fork or stick to release some of the steam. Open carefully so you don't burn yourself. Transfer the popcorn to a serving bowl or keep in the pie plate. Drizzle the melted butter over the popcorn; add the crumbled seaweed, nutritional yeast (if using), and smoked sea salt; and toss together.

4   Pass around the campfire.

Note: Seaweed snacks vary in flavor and size; choose a 0.35-ounce snack pack of simple "roasted" seaweed.

# CAMP MESS NACHOS

PREP: 5 minutes

COOK: 5 minutes

YIELD: 4 servings

---

1 tablespoon olive oil

4 extra-large handfuls corn
tortilla chips

One 15-ounce can black beans, drained

1 cup Roasted Corn Salsa (page 107)
or store-bought corn salsa

⅔ cup quick pickled red onions
(see page 38) or store-bought
jalapeño pickles

1 cup shredded cheddar cheese

Sliced green onions, hot sauce, and
plain yogurt or sour cream for topping
(optional)

It was the first snowmelt of spring when I discovered I was pregnant, and suddenly I was infatuated with melted cheese and pickles. Firelight Camps had just opened for the season, and I realized I was going to have to master campfire nachos to keep my insatiable appetite in check on busy days. I crammed tortilla chips, shredded cheese, and all manner of fixings onto sheets of foil and melted, toasted, and roasted the whole shebang over low-burning coals. My baby and I weren't the only ones satisfied; our staff and guests loved my mess of ingredients, and I began making extra to share. This recipe is for four individual but shareable portions. For meat lovers, top with cooked ground beef or pork.

---

1   Fire the grill to medium heat, or let the campfire burn low so the coals are red and glowing at medium heat. Position the grill grate 6 inches above the coals.

2   Put four 12-inch sheets of aluminum foil on a flat surface and grease with the olive oil. Place a generous handful of tortilla chips in the center of each foil sheet. Divide the black beans, salsa, and pickled onions evenly over each pile of chips. Sprinkle ¼ cup of the cheese over each serving.

3   Fold up two sides of the foil to meet in the middle and fold the edges over each other to seal the top. Then fold the two open ends of the foil to seal the packet. Place the foil packets over direct heat and cook for about 5 minutes. Open the packets carefully to allow steam to escape. If the cheese is not melted, return to the heat for a few minutes more before digging in.

4   Serve the nachos directly from the foil—fewer plates to clean!—and top with green onions, hot sauce, and a dollop of yogurt, if desired. Demolish these—leftovers don't keep well.

Note: To prepare at home, preheat the oven to 350°F. Line a rimmed baking sheet or dish with aluminum foil and assemble the nachos as directed. Bake for about 10 minutes, until cheese is melted.

# PIGGIES IN PAJAMAS

PREP: 15 minutes

COOK: 5 to 10 minutes

YIELD: 4 to 6 servings

---

All-purpose flour for dusting

1 recipe Quick Campfire Puff Pastry (page 114)

¼ cup Zesty Za'atar (see page 33; optional)

30 precooked cocktail wieners or 10 hot dogs, cut into thirds

Note: To bake your piggies at home, preheat the oven to 400°F. Line a rimmed baking sheet with parchment paper and arrange the pigs in rows, spacing them about 1 inch apart. Bake for 15 minutes, then lower the oven temperature to 350°F and continue to bake until toasted brown and puffed, about 15 minutes more.

Homemade dough and a generous shower of Zesty Za'atar make these quintessential campfire morsels better than any you've ever had. You can bake them over the campfire using long bamboo skewers or whittled sticks, or prebake them at home (see Note) and simply warm them over the flames. You can swap in 1½ boxes store-bought puff pastry; just be sure to choose one made with all butter and no substitutes like shortening, which sacrifices the flavor. Dress these piggies up with the Best Ketchup on Earth (page 30) and Whole-Grain Honey Mustard (page 31); dunking them right on the stick. For hot dogs with tougher skins, peel off the skin to prevent the wiener from sliding out of the dough when you take a bite.

---

PREP Line a large airtight container with parchment paper. Lightly dust a work surface and a rolling pin with all-purpose flour.

Place one piece of the chilled pastry on the prepared work surface and roll into a 16 by 7-inch rectangle about ⅛ inch thick. Mark points 2 inches apart along one long edge of the rectangle. The 2-inch space will be the base of a triangle; from both points, using a pizza wheel or sharp knife, slice on a diagonal toward the other side, meeting in a midpoint on the opposite edge. Repeat. You will end up with fifteen triangles and two half-triangles. Repeat with the second piece of dough. (Save the half triangles for Snakes on a Stick; see variation.)

Evenly dust the dough with the za'atar.

Place a cocktail wiener at the wide end of a triangle and roll the dough entirely around the wiener, ending with the point of the triangle on the outside. Transfer to the prepared container and repeat with the remaining wieners and dough, leaving about ¼ inch of space between pigs in the container. Place a sheet of parchment paper on top of the finished pigs before adding a new layer in order to prevent them from sticking to each other. Seal the container and then chill for up to 2 days.

1. Build a campfire and let the coals burn down until red and glowing at medium heat. When cooking your pigs over the fire, patience is key.

2. One at a time, push a skewer into the end of an assembled pig and hold it over the coals. Rotate the skewer slowly and evenly until the dough puffs up and turns golden brown, about 10 minutes. (If you prebaked your pigs, it will take only 2 to 3 minutes to reheat over the fire.)

3. Serve warm. Store leftovers in an airtight container or ziplock bag, chilled, for up to 4 days.

## VARIATION

For Snakes on a Stick, bypass the pigs and roll the dough into 4 by 1-inch ropes. Push a skewer into one end of a rope and coil the rope around the skewer (like a snake), pinching the end of the dough together to secure it on the stick. For a savory option, roll the rope in Zesty Za'atar. For a dessert option, brush melted butter over the dough and sprinkle ½ teaspoon ground cinnamon and ½ teaspoon sugar over the top. Proceed as directed.

# QUICK CAMPFIRE PUFF PASTRY

PREP: 25 minutes

COOK: None

YIELD: About 1½ pounds

---

1 cup unbleached all-purpose flour, plus more for dusting

1 cup whole-wheat flour

1 teaspoon fine salt

1½ cups plus 2 tablespoons unsalted butter, cold and straight from the fridge

½ cup ice-cold water (see Note)

A camping cookbook would be incomplete without a recipe for pigs in a blanket, a campfire standard that is, after all, nothing more than a fancy version of a wiener on a stick. I searched through dozens of cookbooks for a recipe that uses homemade dough and found nothing. Exasperated by this void, I turned to my friends Shanti and Steve, owners of Talula's Pizza in Asbury Park, New Jersey, and dough connoisseurs, to help fulfill my dreams of mouth-filling, flaky, fluffy pajamas for my piggies. Together we figured out a foolproof method for quick puff pastry. The advantage of homemade puff pastry is that you can make it with high-quality butter, preferably made with milk from grass-fed cows, which results in a more tender, utterly buttery dough that crisps perfectly over the campfire. This dough is entirely made at home; double or triple the recipe so you have extra on-hand for all your adventures.

---

1  Dust a clean surface and rolling pin with all-purpose flour.

2  In the bowl of a stand mixer or a large bowl, combine both flours and the salt and mix with a fork.

3  Using a pastry cutter or sharp paring knife, chop the butter into ½-inch cubes and add it to the flour. (Don't worry about being too precise with the size of your butter cubes.)

4  Fit the mixer with the paddle attachment and mix on low speed until the butter is just incorporated into the flour, about 30 seconds. Or, use your hands to quickly work the butter into the flour, just until incorporated. The cubes of butter should still be about the same size, just slightly mashed with the flour. You do not want your flour to look like coarse bread crumbs.

5  With the mixer still on low speed. Add the ice-cold water to the flour mixture a spoonful at a time, and continue to beat until the dough comes together into a crumbly, sticky ball. Alternatively, mix the dough together with a fork. Turn the dough out onto your floured surface.

Note: To make ice-cold water, add 2 ice cubes to water and let sit for a few minutes. Remove the ice cubes before adding the water to the dough.

6   Pat the dough into a rough 5 by 8-inch rectangle. Fold the dough like a business letter, with the bottom third toward the middle and the upper third over the first fold. Turn the dough 90 degrees. Pat the dough into a 1-inch-thick rectangle and repeat this fold twice more, a total of three times, patting the dough back into a 1-inch-thick rectangle between folds. If the dough sticks to the work surface, lightly dust with more all-purpose flour as needed.

7   Divide the dough in half and press and flatten each half into smaller 3½ by 6-inch rectangles, about 1 inch thick. Wrap one half in plastic wrap and let chill while you prepare the other half.

8   Roll out one piece of dough into a 5 by 8-inch rectangle, about ½ inch thick. Repeat the business-letter fold, with the bottom third toward the middle and the upper third over that. Turn the dough 90 degrees. Pat the dough into a 1-inch-thick rectangle and repeat this fold another three times with the rolling pin, flattening the dough back into a 1-inch-thick rectangle between folds. You will make a total of seven folds.

9   Once you've finished your last fold, shape the dough into a 3½ by 6-inch rectangle again and cover tightly with plastic wrap. Repeat with the second piece of dough.

10  Chill the puff pastry for up to 3 days before cooking, or freeze for up to 1 month.

**explore**

# SIDES

These recipes are designed as dishes to pass, and make the perfect complement to your entrees. Ask friends and family to take charge of a side dish, and save leftovers for breakfast or picnic lunch.

# RED PEPPER– FENNEL KRAUT

PREP: 7 minutes

COOK: 10 minutes

YIELD: 4 to 6 servings

---

1 red bell pepper

1 fennel bulb

2 slices nitrate-free bacon (see Note, page 71), coarsely chopped

1 cup sauerkraut

This German-style kraut is lightly cooked with bacon bits and embellished with the rich, anise flavor of fennel and the fresh snap of red bell pepper. Save extra bacon fat and kraut for scrambling with eggs, topping coal-baked potatoes (see page 123), or scattering onto Grilled Hawaiian Pizza (page 140) with sausage.

---

**PREP** Seed the bell pepper and slice very thinly. Halve and core the fennel and then slice very thinly. Combine the bell pepper and fennel in a large ziplock bag or airtight container and then chill for up to 3 days.

1   Line a plate with paper towels.

2   Add the bacon to a cold 10-inch cast-iron skillet or frying pan and set over medium heat. Cook until the bacon is brown and crispy, about 8 minutes total, flipping every 2 minutes with tongs. (Cooking time will vary depending on the thickness of your bacon; the key is to keep a close eye on it.) Transfer the bacon to the prepared plate to let the paper towel absorb the excess grease. Pour the bacon fat from the pan into a small mason jar, leaving a film on the pan. (Cool, seal, and chill the bacon fat for up to 6 months to use for frying eggs or roasting potatoes.) Do not rinse the pan.

3   Once the bacon has cooled, crumble it into smaller pieces and return it to the pan. Using tongs, toss in the bell pepper and fennel and cook until soft and tender, about 5 minutes. Toss in the sauerkraut and cook until heated through, about 2 minutes, then remove from the heat.

4   Serve warm or cold. Store leftovers in an airtight container, chilled, for up to 5 days.

Every summer, Mamma moved her cooking to the backyard grill as soon as the weather was nice. She would collect the enormous eggplants and zucchini from her garden, slice them thinly, bathe them with olive oil, and char them on the grill. It was such an easy, flavorful side dish that preserved the vegetables' essence with just a little nudge from the fire and smoke. You can prepare a number of vegetables the same way, including bell peppers, broccoli, and tomatoes. Keep in mind that each vegetable requires a different cooking time. Save leftovers for making grilled vegetable and hummus sandwiches (see page 76) or adding to a frittata (see page 67). The cut eggplant will brown slightly before arriving at camp, but it won't affect the flavor. If bringing a colander, you can also prepare the entire recipe at camp.

**PREP** Cut the eggplant lengthwise into ¼-inch slices and place in a colander. Coat with 2 tablespoons salt and set the colander over a plate, bowl, or sink for 15 to 30 minutes to drain the bitter juices. Rinse the eggplant and pat dry with a paper towel or a tea towel.

Cut the zucchini lengthwise into ¼-inch slices. Transfer the vegetables to one or two large ziplock bags.

In a small bowl, whisk together the ¼ cup olive oil, pepper, and 2 teaspoons salt; add to the vegetables in the bag(s); and seal. Use your hands to evenly coat the vegetables with the oil and then chill for up to 24 hours.

1   Fire the grill or campfire to high heat and position the grill grate 4 inches above the coals. If using parsley, remove the leaves from the stems and finely chop the leaves.

2   Remove the vegetables from the bag(s) and, using tongs, place them over direct heat and cook until the first side is charred, 5 to 7 minutes. If you like your vegetables crispy (like me), cook them as long as you want. Flip the vegetables carefully so they don't fall through the grate, and then char on the other side, 3 to 5 minutes more. Transfer the grilled vegetables to a baking sheet or serving dish, or directly onto each camper's plate. Drizzle the vegetables with olive oil and sprinkle the parsley and za'atar over the top.

3   Serve warm, at ambient temperature, or cold. Store leftovers in an airtight container, chilled, for up to 5 days.

# GRILLED EGGPLANT AND ZUCCHINI WITH ZESTY ZA'ATAR

PREP: 15 minutes
COOK: 10 to 30 minutes
YIELD: 4 to 6 servings

1 large eggplant (see Note)
Kosher salt
2 large zucchini
¼ cup olive oil, plus more for drizzling
20 turns of the pepper mill
4 leafy parsley sprigs (optional)
¼ cup Zesty Za'atar (see page 33)

Note: When shopping, look for an eggplant with skin that's shiny and smooth, without any wrinkles.

To roast the vegetables at home, preheat the oven to 450°F. Line a large, rimmed baking sheet with aluminum foil. Spread the vegetables evenly on the baking sheet and bake, tossing halfway through cooking, until browned, tender, and shrunken in size, about 30 minutes.

# GRILLED ASPARAGUS WITH HONEY MUSTARD DRESSING AND SHAVED PARMESAN

PREP: 5 minutes
COOK: 10 minutes
YIELD: 4 servings

---

2 pounds asparagus

1 tablespoon olive oil

½ teaspoon kosher salt

20 turns of the pepper mill

⅓ cup Honey Mustard Dressing (see page 87)

Parmesan wedge for garnish

When chef and author Simon Majumdar announced his tour "Give Us A Bed I'll Cook You Dinner," I immediately invited him to Firelight Camps. I had one caveat. I wanted to cook a campfire feast *with* him for our guests. He arrived in May, when fresh produce is still hard to come by. Our menu planning took on the appearance of a reality TV challenge: Prepare five unforgettable dishes with ten available ingredients. Go! We set off on a treasure hunt to all my favorite farms, scrounging what we could. Melissa Madden, farmer and owner of the Good Life Farm, gave us her first harvest of asparagus, which is like green gold to the winter-starved diet! We paired this dish with her Workhorse hard cider, named for the draft horses that till the alleys between the apple trees where the asparagus grows.

---

1 Fire the grill to medium-high heat and position the grill grate 2 to 4 inches above the coals.

2 While the asparagus are still bundled, slice off about 2 inches from the fibrous bottoms.

3 Rinse the asparagus, allowing a few water droplets to cling to the stalks, and transfer to a serving plate or baking sheet; the moisture will help them steam and cook over the fire. Add the olive oil and, using long tongs or your hands, toss the asparagus until evenly coated with the oil. Season with the salt and pepper.

4 Place the asparagus on the grill grate over direct heat. Using long tongs, rotate the asparagus frequently and cook until tender and charred, 5 to 10 minutes. Be careful not to let any fall through the grate.

5 Transfer the grilled asparagus to a serving plate, baking sheet, or campers' plates and drizzle with the dressing. Set out the Parmesan wedge with a vegetable peeler so campers can add thin shavings of cheese to their dish.

6 Serve warm or cold. Store leftovers in an airtight container, chilled, for up to 4 days.

# FIRE-LICKED KALE WITH MAPLE-TAHINI DRESSING

PREP: 10 minutes
COOK: 1 to 2 minutes
YIELD: 4 servings

### MAPLE-TAHINI DRESSING

½ cup tahini, stirred

¼ cup olive oil

¼ cup freshly squeezed lemon juice

¼ cup apple cider vinegar

2 tablespoons maple syrup

1 teaspoon kosher salt

8 turns of the pepper mill

1 tablespoon warm water (optional)

1 bunch kale, any variety

Olive oil for drizzling

This fire-licked kale is always the winning dish at my campfire meals. The primal wood smoke and charred swaths of kale are ravishing, but the method couldn't be simpler. All you need is a hot grill, hearty greens, olive oil, and two minutes of cooking time. Collards, chard, radicchio, and escarole are also good camping greens because they don't bruise or wilt easily. Try this method with escarole, topped with olive oil, shaved Parmesan, shaved apple, and toasted walnuts; or grilled chard with balsamic vinegar, sliced plums, and Maple-Rosemary Roasted Almond Mix (page 39). The kale is equally delicious served cold.

If you're feeling ambitious, lay a grill grate sturdily over a medium-high campfire and cook the kale on top as described; be sure to wear welding gloves to protect your hands.

---

**PREP** To make the dressing: In a lidded jar, combine the tahini, olive oil, lemon juice, vinegar, maple syrup, salt, and pepper. Seal tightly and shake vigorously until incorporated, about 30 seconds. (For a smoother, lighter consistency, make the dressing with a blender.) For a thinner dressing, add the warm water. Chill for up to 1 month.

1   Fire the grill to medium-high heat and position the grill grate 4 inches above the coals.

2   Place the kale leaves in a large bowl or on a baking sheet and drizzle liberally with olive oil. Use your hands to evenly coat the leaves with the oil.

3   Using long tongs, place the kale leaves, in batches if necessary, on the grill grate in a single layer. The flames will jump up and lick the kale, charring the leaves. Flip the kale leaves as soon as they become charred, 30 to 60 seconds, and cook the other side, 30 to 60 seconds more. Transfer the kale to a cutting board and, once cool, strip the leaves from the stems; compost the stems. Using a sharp chef's knife, cut the leaves into ribbons. Transfer to a serving bowl or campers' plates, drizzling liberally with the dressing.

4   Serve immediately. Store leftovers in an airtight container, chilled, for up to 5 days.

With this quick recipe you can have potatoes in time for dinner without washing off the soot; and you can replace russet potatoes with yams or sweet potatoes. Add your favorite herbs and spices to season your foil-packet potatoes—I love a spoonful of Basil–Sunflower Seed Pesto (page 80) or Zesty Za'atar (see page 33). The fixings bar makes this especially fun and customizable for all ages, turning a simple potato into a hearty side or entrée. Save a few strips of crispy bacon from your Zesty "Praline" Bacon (page 60) or Chocolate, Bacon, and Burrata Breakfast Sandwich (page 71) and crush into bacon bits for topping.

**PREP** In a lidded bowl or ziplock bag, combine the potatoes, olive oil, salt, and pepper; toss together or seal the bag and massage with your hands to evenly coat the potatoes with oil; and then chill for up to 24 hours. (The potatoes may brown a little, but it won't affect the flavor of your dish.)

1   Put four 12-inch sheets of aluminum foil on a flat surface. Divide the potatoes among the foil sheets, mounding them in the center. Fold up two sides of the foil to meet in the middle and fold the edges over each other to seal the top. Then fold the two open ends of the foil to seal the packet.

2   *To cook the packets on the grill:* Fire the grill to medium-high heat and position the grill grate 2 inches above the coals. Place the foil packets over direct heat and cook for 45 minutes. Rotate the packets with tongs every 10 to 15 minutes.

   *To cook the packets on the campfire:* Let the coals burn down to medium-high heat. Use a shovel to create wells in the coals and place the foil packets inside. Cover with coals and cook for 45 minutes. Move the coals with the shovel and use tongs to pull out the packets.

3   While the potatoes are cooking, line up the pickled onions, cheese, yogurt, and green onions on the table so it's easy for campers to add their own toppings.

4   Open the foil packets carefully to let steam escape. Use a fork to check if the potatoes are tender. If not, cook for 5 to 15 minutes more. Let cool enough to handle.

5   Serve directly from the foil—fewer plates to clean! Store leftovers in an airtight container, chilled, for up to 5 days.

# COAL-BAKED POTATOES AND FIXINGS

**PREP:** 5 minutes
**COOK:** 45 to 60 minutes
**YIELD:** 4 servings

4 russet potatoes, halved lengthwise and cut into ¼-inch slices

2 tablespoons olive oil

2 teaspoons salt

20 turns of the pepper mill

1 cup quick pickled red onions (see page 38) or store-bought pickled jalapeños, 1 cup shredded cheddar cheese, ½ cup plain yogurt or sour cream, and/or ½ cup thinly sliced green onions

Note: To cook the packets in an oven, bake at 350°F for 1 hour.

Known for its vibrant Afro-Ecuadorian community, the valley of El Chota is tucked in the mountainous north of Ecuador. It's a surreal, desert oasis brimming with soul. I visited during Carnaval, with its enthusiastic water fights. To stay dry from the deluge, I spent most of my time seeking shelter in the market stalls on the festival grounds. This is how I discovered the most luscious grilled corn on the cob I had ever tasted. Instead of butter, the corn is slathered with a creamy chile-lime sauce that adds just the right amount of tang and spice.

**PREP** Finely grate the zest of the lime and set aside. Cut the lime into wedges and juice as many wedges as you need to yield 1 teaspoon lime juice.

In a lidded jar or airtight container, combine the feta, yogurt, mayonnaise, red pepper flakes, lime zest, and lime juice and stir to mix. Seal the jar and then chill for up to 3 days.

Pack the remaining lime wedges in a ziplock bag and chill for up to 3 days.

1   Fire the grill or campfire to medium-high heat and position the grill grate 2 to 4 inches above the coals.

2   Place the ears of corn over direct heat and, using tongs, rotate every 2 to 3 minutes until the ears are uniformly charred and the kernels bright yellow, 10 to 12 minutes. For a darker char, drizzle olive oil over the corn so it drips onto the coals and the flames jump up to lick the corn.

3   Transfer the corn to a serving plate or baking sheet. Shake the feta mixture to reincorporate and then spread evenly over each ear of corn and sprinkle with the cilantro.

4   Serve immediately with the lime wedges. This is the kind of finger food you just dig in to and get messy—you'll have cheese on your face and corn in your teeth but it's so good you'll be grinning ear to ear.

# CHILE-LIME FESTIVAL CORN WITH FETA AND CILANTRO

PREP: About 5 minutes
COOK: About 8 minutes
YIELD: 6 servings

1 lime
¾ cup finely crumbled feta
½ cup plain yogurt
¼ cup mayonnaise (see page 32)
1 teaspoon red pepper flakes
6 ears corn (see Note), shucked
Olive oil for drizzling (optional)
¼ cup finely chopped fresh cilantro

Note: When buying corn, look for bright green husks that are wrapped tightly around the ears. Pull back the husk an inch to see if neat rows of kernels adorn the tip. Pop a kernel with your thumbnail to see if it releases milky sap—if so, scoop it up!

sides

# DUTCH OVEN ROSEMARY– SEA SALT CORNBREAD WITH HARD-CIDER BUTTER

PREP: 7 minutes

COOK: 25 minutes

YIELD: 6 to 8 servings

---

1¼ cups coarse cornmeal

1 cup unbleached all-purpose flour

2 tablespoons minced fresh rosemary

1 tablespoon aluminum-free baking powder

1 teaspoon fine salt

One 14.75-ounce can creamed-style corn

½ cup melted unsalted butter, plus 1 tablespoon

2 eggs

½ teaspoon coarse sea salt (preferably sel gris)

Hard-Cider Butter (recipe follows) for serving

When I think of cast iron, I think of cornbread, and there's nothing quite like Dutch oven cornbread baked over a fire. I adapted this from a recipe by Nealey Dozier of theKitchn.com; her addition of creamed-style corn makes cornbread that is perfectly moist. But the real trick is to sizzle butter in the Dutch oven before adding the batter. This will help form a crisp, toasted crust and give you a cornbread that doesn't fall apart. I love the garden-fresh aroma of rosemary combined with flecks of coarse sea salt, though you can play with other combinations, such as lemon zest and thyme. You will need a 10-inch Dutch oven with a lid (ideally a flanged lid). To make this gluten-free, simply substitute with a gluten-free all-purpose flour.

---

**PREP** In a ziplock bag, combine the cornmeal, flour, rosemary, baking powder, and fine salt and store in a cool, dark place for up to 2 days.

In a large lidded jar or airtight container, combine the corn, ½ cup melted butter, and eggs. Seal the jar or container, shake vigorously until incorporated, about 30 seconds, and then chill for up to 24 hours.

1   Fire the grill or campfire to medium-high heat and position the grill grate 6 inches above the coals.

2   In a large bowl, combine the wet ingredients with the dry ingredients and stir together until a batter forms.

3   Place a 10-inch Dutch oven on the grill grate over direct heat, melt the remaining 1 tablespoon unsalted butter, and tilt the pot to coat the bottom and sides. Once the butter begins to foam (before it browns!), pour in the batter and sprinkle with the sea salt. Cover the Dutch oven and use tongs to transfer an even layer of hot coals onto the lid, so that it is barely visible. This will create an oven effect. As the coals turn to ash or lose heat, add more hot coals to keep the temperature on the lid at medium heat.

4   Cook until the cornbread is toasted brown around the edges and golden-brown on the surface, 20 to 25 minutes; the smell of sweet cornbread filling the air will signal when it's ready. Use your Dutch oven's lid-lifter to remove the lid with hot coals carefully and check to see if the cornbread is done. (If you are not using a flanged lid, the hot coals need to be removed first or they will spill

into the cornbread. Remove them carefully with tongs and blow ash off the lid—away from people—then use your lid-lifter to remove the lid.) If the cornbread needs more time, replace the lid and coals, and cook for 5 minutes more. When ready, cut the cornbread into wedges or squares.

5   Serve warm, directly from the Dutch oven, alongside Hard-Cider Butter for campers to add themselves. (Be sure to warn your fellow campers that the pot is hot!) Store leftovers in an airtight container at ambient temperature for up to 5 days.

In the Finger Lakes region, both cultivated and wild apple trees flank farms, roads, and deep woods trails. As a result, I have all manner of apple products in my kitchen year-round, including fresh apples and hard apple cider. This reduction of the two is otherworldly. It's a velvety, rich, spreadable version of applesauce intended for lathering on cornbread or swirling into yogurt for breakfast or dessert. The alcohol is cooked off, making this kid-friendly too.

1   In a large pot, combine the apples, apple cider, and maple syrup. Bring to a boil, then lower to a simmer and cook, uncovered, until the apples are tender, about 20 minutes. Let cool and then transfer to a food processor (or use an immersion blender) and whiz into a silky-smooth sauce. Return the apple mixture to the pot over low heat and add the butter and pumpkin spice, stirring until the butter is completely melted.

2   Store in an airtight container, chilled, for up to 1 week; it will firm up once chilled.

# HARD-CIDER BUTTER

PREP: 10 minutes
COOK: 25 minutes
YIELD: 2 cups

5 apples, peeled, cored, and cut into ½-inch cubes

1 cup hard apple cider

¼ cup maple syrup

3 tablespoons unsalted butter

¼ teaspoon pumpkin spice

## MAIN
## EVENTS

Far from the crutch of a pantry
or store, eating outside makes
food come alive and connects
us around the truly unique
human activity of cooking a
meal. The family-style dishes
in this section will make you
feel at home in the wild.

# "WELCOME TO THE GARDEN" THAI CURRY

PREP: 15 minutes

COOK: 45 minutes

YIELD: 6 servings

---

1 tablespoon coconut oil

1 medium yellow onion, thinly sliced

1 tablespoon minced garlic

1-inch piece fresh ginger, peeled and grated

3 tablespoons Thai red curry paste

One 14-ounce can coconut milk (see Note, page 172)

½ cup water

1 to 2 tablespoons fish sauce, or 1 teaspoon kosher salt

2 medium carrots, thinly sliced

1 large yellow potato, cut into 1-inch cubes

One 20-ounce can pineapple chunks, drained (see Note, page 140)

2 cups frozen peas (see Note)

½ cup seeded and diced red bell pepper

1 handful fresh Thai or Italian basil

3 cups cooked instant brown rice

2 limes, quartered

1 jalapeño chile, seeded and thinly sliced (optional)

My twin sister and I first created this pineapple curry on Christmas Eve in Prague, the first stop on a three-week backpacking trip through Eastern Europe with friends. We weren't the only ones who had chosen to spend the holiday away from home for the first time, and quickly bonded with the other travelers in the youth hostel. That night, we celebrated like family, sharing a huge pot of curry, bottles of wine, and travel stories. Several years later, my husband and I opened our own hostel and café in Nicaragua, La Buena Onda, and I wasn't surprised when this curry became the signature dish on the menu. Pineapple is the global symbol for hospitality, and adds a delicate sweetness to this colorful Thai curry, which will make anyone—anywhere—feel welcome and well fed. Buy pineapple chunks in a can that contains only pineapple and pineapple juice. If the carrots are organic, don't peel the skin—it's the most nutritious part! I like to use Thai Kitchen brand red curry paste.

---

1   In a 12-inch cast-iron skillet or sauté pan over medium heat, melt the coconut oil. Add the onion, garlic, and ginger and sauté until the onion is translucent and soft, about 5 minutes. Stir in the curry paste.

2   Add half of the coconut milk, the water, and 1 tablespoon of the fish sauce to the pan. Stir in the carrots and potato and gently simmer. Turn the heat to medium-low, cover, and simmer until the vegetables are tender, about 12 minutes. Add the pineapple, peas, bell pepper, and remaining coconut milk to the pan and stir to combine. Taste, and add the remaining 1 tablespoon fish sauce if needed. Bring back to a simmer and cook, uncovered, for 3 minutes more. Remove the pan from the heat and stir in the basil.

3   Fill the bottom of each camper's bowl with rice and ladle the curry over the top. Place the lime quarters and jalapeño (if using) on the table so campers can garnish as desired.

4   Serve immediately. Store leftovers in an airtight container, chilled, for up to 4 days.

Note: Pack frozen peas directly into the cooler; they will double as an ice pack.

My friend Katie is a uniquely talented florist whose bouquets bring delight to thousands of guests every season at Firelight Camps. For her bachelorette party, we lined our grazing tables with brightly painted tin cans and filled them with colorful stems, then crafted a vegetarian potluck that capitalized on summer's bounty. This dish was my contribution, and it's so hearty it would be welcome at any celebration.

**PREP** Place the coconut in a small pan and toast over medium heat until lightly browned, 3 to 5 minutes. Do not leave the coconut unattended or it *will* burn. Transfer immediately to a plate or bowl to cool. Transfer to a ziplock bag or airtight container and then chill for up to 6 months.

Squeeze excess water from the tofu by sandwiching the slices between two kitchen towels or thick paper towels on a firm surface. Place a baking sheet on top and use your hands to press down firmly for five slow counts. Repeat with another set of dry towels. Transfer the tofu to an airtight container to protect it once packed in the cooler, and then chill for up to 24 hours.

1. Fire the grill or campfire to medium heat and position the grill grate 4 inches above the coals.

2. Add the coconut oil to the tofu in the container, and use your hands to gently toss and evenly coat the tofu.

3. Using tongs, place the tofu over direct heat and cook until the outer skin is crispy with grill marks, about 5 minutes per side.

4. Transfer the tofu to a serving plate, baking sheet, or bowl and toss with the barbecue sauce and ¼ cup of the coconut. For a beautiful presentation, layer the tofu like dominoes and garnish with the remaining 2 tablespoons shredded coconut.

5. Serve immediately. Store leftovers in an airtight container, chilled, for up to 4 days.

# BBQ TOFU WITH TOASTED COCONUT

PREP: 10 minutes
COOK: 10 minutes
YIELD: 4 servings

**¼ cup plus 2 tablespoons shredded coconut**

**One 14-ounce block extra-firm tofu, cut vertically into ½-inch slices**

**¼ cup coconut oil, melted**

**½ cup barbecue sauce**

Note: To cook on a camp stove, in a 12-inch cast-iron skillet or pan over medium-high heat, warm the coconut oil. When the oil is hot, add the tofu, lightly frying until the skin is crispy and golden in color, about 5 minutes per side.

main events

My Mexicana soul-sister, Ana, created this vegetarian recipe when she couldn't stand one more taco with just rice and beans. She wanted a nourishing and filling alternative that gave her clear energy. As she started learning more about Ayurveda, a holistic approach to eating, she boosted her recipe with flavorful spices. The secret in this simple taco lies in the method in which it's prepared. For a truly Ayurvedic dish, use ghee (clarified butter), which is becoming more widely stocked in grocery stores and available online. And of course, don't forget your toppings.

**PREP** In a 12-inch cast-iron skillet or sauté pan over high heat, combine the sweet potatoes and enough cold water to cover. Bring to a gentle boil, then cover and cook until fork-tender, 6 to 8 minutes. Drain and let cool.

Pack the sweet potatoes, garlic, and 1 tablespoon of the butter in a ziplock bag or airtight container and then chill for up to 3 days.

Pack the onion and 1 tablespoon butter in a ziplock bag or airtight container and then chill for up to 24 hours.

Combine the cumin, coriander seeds, garam masala, and pepper in a ziplock bag or airtight container and store in a cool, dark place for up to 2 weeks.

1   In a 12-inch cast-iron skillet over medium heat, melt the remaining 3 tablespoons butter. Once the butter begins to foam (before it browns!), stir in the spice mixture with a wooden spoon. Spread it evenly in the pan and let sizzle until aromatic, about 1 minute. Add the onion-butter mixture, stirring until the butter melts, and sauté until tender, 5 to 7 minutes. Add the sweet potato–garlic mixture, stirring until the butter melts once again, 2 to 3 minutes. Add the kale, toss with tongs, and cook until the kale turns bright green and wilts, about 2 minutes more. Remove the pan from the heat and toss in the salt.

2   Serve the sweet potato filling warm, directly from the pan (be sure to warn your fellow campers that the pan is hot!) alongside the tortillas and toppings on a table so campers can assemble their own tacos, squeezing the lime over the top. Store leftovers in an airtight container, chilled, for up to 3 days. Add a splash of water when reheating.

# SPICED SWEET POTATO AND KALE TACOS

**PREP:** 15 minutes
**COOK:** 25 minutes
**YIELD:** 6 servings

2 large sweet potatoes, cut into ½-inch cubes

3 garlic cloves, minced or grated

5 tablespoons unsalted butter, ghee, coconut oil, or olive oil

1 red onion, halved and thinly sliced

2 tablespoons ground cumin

1½ tablespoons toasted coriander seeds, crushed

¼ teaspoon garam masala or ground cinnamon

20 turns of the pepper mill

5 cups thinly sliced kale leaves

½ teaspoon kosher salt

12 small corn tortillas, warmed (see Note)

Sliced avocado or Guacamole in Its Shell (page 103), crumbled goat cheese or feta, plain yogurt or sour cream, chopped fresh cilantro, salsa or diced tomatoes, and/or hot sauce for topping

1 lime, sliced

Note: To warm tortillas on the grill, brush the tortillas with olive oil and grill directly over medium-high heat until lightly charred. To warm tortillas on the stove top, add them one at a time to a pan over low heat, flipping once or twice. Transfer to a plate and wrap with a damp tea towel to keep moist and warm until ready to serve; they will break less easily once filled.

main events

# BEST VEGGIE BURGER

PREP: 45 minutes
COOK: 40 minutes
YIELD: 12 servings

---

1 cup cooked instant brown rice

2 cups peeled, shredded beets

2 cups shredded carrots

1 cup minced onion

1 cup finely chopped fresh parsley

1 garlic clove, minced

1 cup shredded cheddar cheese

1 cup toasted sunflower seeds

½ cup oat flour, rye flour, or any
gluten-free flour

½ cup sunflower oil or other vegetable
oil, plus 1 tablespoon (optional)

2 eggs, lightly beaten

2 tablespoons tamari or soy sauce

1 teaspoon kosher salt

½ teaspoon freshly ground
black pepper

College dining turned me into a vegetarian for six years. The cafeteria food was overprocessed, oversalted, and delivered from who knows where. But it turned out that finding a veggie burger that wasn't masquerading as beef, or even worse, collapsing into a pile of black beans, was harder than finding a needle in a haystack. If I wanted a rich, moist, flavorful veggie burger that was going to stick together, I was going to have to make it myself. With a little help from *Farmer John's Cookbook*, after months of trial and error, I finally created a veggie burger that even my meat-loving sister Francesca will devour. These burgers are prepared in advance at home, and reheated at camp. The recipe makes 12 patties, but sometimes I like to form smaller patties or sliders. It does take some effort, so I've included my favorite shortcut: instant brown rice. This saves 30 to 45 minutes of cooking time, yielding the same nutritional value and often better texture. You can also save time with a food processor by processing the beets and carrots with the shredding disc instead of a box grater. If the carrots are organic, don't peel the skin—it's the most nutritious part! You can serve the veggie burgers over a salad, sandwiched in a bun, or between Charred Bread (page 102) with Best Ketchup on Earth (page 30), Whole-Grain Honey Mustard (page 31), or Smoked Paprika Aioli (see variation, page 32).

---

**PREP** Line a baking sheet with a paper towel.

In a large bowl, combine the rice, beets, carrots, onion, parsley, garlic, cheese, sunflower seeds, oat flour, ½ cup sunflower oil, eggs, tamari, salt, and pepper. Use your hands to mix thoroughly. To absorb some of the moisture from the beets and carrots, spread the vegetable mixture in an even layer on the prepared baking sheet and refrigerate for at least 15 minutes or up to 2 hours.

Preheat the oven to 350°F.

Remove the vegetable mixture from the refrigerator. With the palms of your hands, shape about ¼ cup of the mixture into a patty and place on a second rimmed baking sheet. Repeat until you've used all the mixture to form 12 patties, placing them about 1 inch apart.

continued

Bake the veggie burgers until the edges begin to brown, about 25 minutes.

Let cool completely. Store in an airtight container, chilled, for up to 3 days, or cover each patty with plastic wrap, place in a large ziplock bag, and freeze for up to 3 months. (They will double as ice in your cooler!)

1   If the patties are frozen, remove them from the cooler about 1 hour before you plan to cook them.

2   Fire the grill or campfire to medium heat and position the grill grate 4 inches above the coals. Cook the patties over direct heat until slightly charred and warmed through, 1 to 2 minutes per side. Alternatively, on a camp stove, in a skillet over medium heat, warm the 1 teaspoon sunflower oil. Add the patties, working in batches if necessary and adding 1 teaspoon oil in between, and cook until browned on each side and warmed through, 3 to 4 minutes per side. (It will take a little bit longer in the pan than on the grill.)

3   Serve warm. Store leftovers in an airtight container, chilled, for up to 3 days.

One of my earliest kitchen memories is standing on a chair at the counter and shaping Italian *polpettine* (meatballs) with my mother. This burger is a jumbo *polpettina*, succulent and bursting with flavor. I love this recipe because it's easy to do and you can double or triple the quantity to freeze a batch for another night. If making burgers, this recipe yields four jumbo patties, but you can stretch it out to make about twelve meatballs. If you plan to make these as meatballs, serve them over spaghetti with Homemade Marinara Sauce (page 151). If you have a food processor, use it to mince the onion, garlic, and parsley for quicker preparation.

**PREP** In a large bowl, combine the beef, onion, garlic, parsley, Parmesan, bread crumbs, egg, salt, and pepper. Use your hands to mix thoroughly, and then form four patties.

Cover each patty with plastic wrap, transfer to a ziplock bag, and then chill for up to 1 day, or freeze for up to 4 months. (They will double as ice in your cooler!)

1   If the patties are frozen, remove them from the cooler about 1 hour before you plan to cook them.

2   *To cook on the grill:* Fire the grill to medium-high heat and position the grill grate 4 inches above the coals. Cook the patties over direct heat for about 2 minutes on one side and then flip, continuing to cook the patties for 2 minutes on the other side. Be attentive or they will burn, in which case, you should move them to indirect heat. Don't be afraid of charring the outside—it adds a flavorful, crispy exterior. After 4 to 5 minutes, the burgers should be medium-rare. Cook longer for medium or well-done; they will become firmer. While the burgers are cooking, toast the hamburger buns over indirect heat.

*To cook on the camp stove:* In a 12-inch cast-iron skillet or frying pan over medium heat, warm the sunflower oil. Add the patties and cook for 3 to 4 minutes per side, flipping with a spatula. When the patties are cooked, drain any fat from the pan into a small jar or container and then toast the buns in the pan.

3   Serve immediately, with the buns. Store leftovers in an airtight container, chilled, for up to 4 days.

# ITALIAN MEATBALL BURGER

PREP: 15 minutes
COOK: 5 minutes
YIELD: 4 servings

1 pound grass-fed ground beef

½ medium yellow onion, minced

1 or 2 garlic cloves, grated

⅔ cup finely chopped fresh parsley

⅓ cup grated Parmesan cheese

¼ cup bread crumbs

1 egg, lightly beaten

1 teaspoon kosher salt

20 grinds of the pepper mill

4 hamburger buns

1 tablespoon sunflower oil or butter (optional)

# GRILLED HAWAIIAN PIZZA

PREP: 25 minutes

PROOF: 18 to 24 hours

COOK: 40 minutes

YIELD: 6 servings

## DOUGH

1¾ cups unbleached all-purpose flour

¼ cup whole-wheat flour

2 teaspoons kosher salt

¼ teaspoon active dry yeast

1½ cups water

1 head broccoli

2 tablespoons olive oil, plus ½ cup

One 20-ounce can pineapple chunks (see Note)

1½ cups marinara sauce (see page 151)

4 cups shredded mozzarella cheese

8 ounces deli ham, sliced into strips or bite-size pieces

Red pepper flakes for garnish (optional)

Note: Choose a can with a pull-tab so you can leave the can opener at home. Add the drained pineapple juice to sparkling water or Hibiscus Lime Power-ade (page 93). You can substitute 2 cups of ½-inch cubes fresh pineapple, peeled and cored. This is about half a medium pine-apple, so chop the rest for snacking at camp, or look for precut fresh pineapple at your grocery store.

Making grilled pizza from scratch is transformational. I discovered this with Shanti and Steve, my dear friends who own Talula's Pizza in Asbury Park, New Jersey. For Steve's thirtieth birthday, Shanti threw a surprise pizza party, taking care to make everything from scratch, from the mozzarella to the dough. At Talula's, they emphasize good-quality, pure flour, which means it isn't bleached, enriched, or bromated. King Arthur is a widely available brand of flour that you can use in your kitchen. It's also important to treat the dough gently—I cannot stress that enough—so that it will hold its character and texture. And don't forget to factor in proofing time (when the dough rises). Finally, the toppings in this recipe were inspired by a family vacation in Hawaii, but you can add whatever toppings your heart desires! I recommend reading through this method twice before diving in. This recipe requires a grill with a lid, so plan on bringing a portable one when you're making this at the campground. If you like, pack extra marinara sauce for dipping your pizza crust!

---

**PREP** To make the dough: In a large bowl combine 1¼ cups of the all-purpose flour, the whole-wheat flour, salt, and yeast and use a fork to mix them together. Add the water and continue to mix until there is no dry flour. Using your hands, gently form the dough into a ball and put into the center of the bowl.

Cover the bowl with plastic wrap or a kitchen towel and let the dough rise at room temperature (about 72°F) until it has more than doubled in size, at least 18 hours in a warm space and up to 24 hours if it is chilly.

Once the dough has risen, scrape onto a lightly floured surface and divide into six equal roughly shaped squares. Working with one piece at a time, pull the right side of the dough toward the center, repeat with the left side, and then the top and bottom—there should be four folds, one from each direction. Then, gently shape the dough into a ball in the palms of your hands and place seam-side down on the floured surface. Repeat with the remaining dough. Dust the balls with additional flour so they are not sticky.

Cover each ball individually with plastic wrap, transfer to an airtight container or ziplock bag (do not rest anything on top), and then chill for up to 3 days.

Pack the remaining ½ cup all-purpose flour in an airtight container for dusting at camp.

Slice the broccoli head lengthwise into 1-inch-thick "steaks." Put the broccoli and 2 tablespoons olive oil in a ziplock bag. Seal the bag, use your hands to evenly coat the broccoli with the oil, and then chill for up to 2 days.

1   Remove the dough from the cooler 2 to 3 hours before you plan to cook the pizzas. Lightly dust two baking sheets with the ½ cup all-purpose flour.

2   Remove the plastic wrap and transfer the balls of dough to a prepared baking sheet. Cover with a damp dish towel and let rest in a cool, shady spot.

3   Drain the pineapple through a crack in the lid or in a tea strainer and transfer the chunks to a bowl. When you're ready to cook, set up a toppings bar with the pineapple, marinara sauce, mozzarella, ham, and broccoli on a table so it's easy to assemble your pizza.

4   Grease the grill grate more thoroughly than usual to be sure the dough doesn't stick. Fire the grill to high heat and position the grill grate 6 inches above the coals.

5   Using tongs, place the broccoli "steaks" over direct heat and cook until evenly charred and tender, 5 to 7 minutes per side. To prevent them from burning, transfer to indirect heat to finish cooking until tender. When done, transfer to a plate or cutting board, let cool slightly, and cut into bite-size pieces. Return to the toppings bar.

6   Now, get ready to grill your pizzas! It's key that you handle the dough gently so you don't push out the natural gases from the fermentation process. Working with one ball of dough at a time, sprinkle with flour and let it hang over the backs of your hands, so it begins to droop and stretch. Transfer the dough to the second prepared baking sheet and use your hands to press the dough into a circle or rectangle that's about ¼ inch thick—the actual edges can be slightly thicker to form a border. Go easy as you stretch the dough, allowing it to retain a bit of unevenness— never use a rolling pin.

continued

7   Using a pastry brush, evenly coat the surface of the dough with 2 teaspoons olive oil. Using your hands, gently pick up the dough and place it on the grill, oiled-side down, first laying one edge of the dough on the grate and then stretching it out flat across the grate, being careful not to touch the scalding grate. Close the grill lid and let the dough cook until it begins to develop charred spots on the bottom, about 2 minutes.

8   Lift the lid and use a spatula to flip the dough on the grill so it is cooked-side up; it will be easy to move now that it is partially cooked. Working quickly, use a spoon to spread ¼ cup marinara sauce over the dough and then top with some of the mozzarella, followed by ham, pineapple, and broccoli. Sprinkle a little more mozzarella over the top to seal everything together. Close the lid and cook until the cheese melts and the bottom of the crust is toasted and charred, about 2 minutes. Repeat with the remaining pizzas. As the pizzas come off the grill, use a sharp knife or pizza cutter to cut into wedges. (If you want to wait to eat together, cover the pizzas with aluminum foil to keep warm, though it just won't be the same as coming right off the grill.)

9   Serve immediately. Make sure the grill master gets first rights to a slice, or they'll all be gone by the time you're done cooking! Set out red pepper flakes so campers can garnish their slice as desired. Store leftovers wrapped in aluminum foil, chilled, for up to 3 days.

My stepfather, Peter, is a devoted student of German language and cuisine and could happily eat sausages and kraut every day of the week. I don't blame him—it's a winning combo! Sausages come neatly packaged for mess-free cooking, and fermented cabbage doesn't spoil easily outdoors. Precooked sausages cook faster and can lessen food-safety worries. I like to serve sausages and kraut over grilled polenta instead of on the traditional bun. You can find plain or flavored tubes of precooked polenta in nearly any grocery store; this is the best option for grilling at camp. Reheat extra polenta and sausages with fried eggs in the morning.

# GRILLED SAUSAGES AND POLENTA WITH RED PEPPER– FENNEL KRAUT

 GF

PREP: 10 minutes
COOK: 20 minutes
YIELD: 4 to 6 servings

One 18-ounce tube polenta, cut into ½-inch-thick slices

2 tablespoons olive oil

½ teaspoon kosher salt

½ teaspoon freshly ground black pepper

8 pork or chicken sausages, any variety

¼ cup Zesty Za'atar (see page 33; optional)

1 recipe Red Pepper–Fennel Kraut (page 118)

1   Fire the grill to high heat and position the grill grate 2 to 4 inches above the coals.

2   Using a pastry brush or spoon, coat both sides of the polenta slices with 1 tablespoon of the olive oil and sprinkle with the salt and pepper.

3   Place the polenta over direct heat. Brush the sausages with the remaining 1 tablespoon olive oil and place them around the polenta. Using a spatula, flip the polenta when the bottoms develop a hardened, charred "skin," 7 to 10 minutes. Continue to cook on the other side until charred, another 7 to 10 minutes.

4   While the polenta is cooking, using tongs, rotate the sausages frequently and cook until browned, 7 to 10 minutes (uncooked sausages will take longer). Because sausages come in varying weights and sizes, slice through the middle of one to check that the interior isn't pink or raw. Use a thermometer to check that the internal temperature has reached 160°F for pork and 165°F for chicken.

5   Transfer the polenta to a serving plate or campers' plates and shower the za'atar (if using) evenly over the top. Pile the sausages and kraut over the polenta.

6   Dig in while hot! Store leftovers in an airtight container, chilled, for up to 3 days.

# SALAMI AND SNAP PEA PAELLA

PREP: 20 minutes
COOK: 40 minutes
YIELD: 4 to 6 servings

---

3 tablespoons olive oil

8 ounces sugar snap peas, cut on a diagonal into ¼-inch slices

½ teaspoon kosher salt

1 medium yellow onion, finely diced

1 large garlic clove, minced

1 cup ¼-inch-cubed, cured salami (see Note)

1 cup Arborio rice

⅓ cup dried wild mushroom pieces (optional)

1 teaspoon smoked paprika

¼ teaspoon ground turmeric

1 pinch saffron (optional)

1½ cups chicken broth or vegetable broth

One 14½-ounce can crushed tomatoes

Finely grated zest of 1 lemon

½ cup sliced or pitted whole green olives (optional)

10 frozen, large shrimp, peeled and deveined with tail on

2 tablespoons finely chopped fresh parsley

1 cup grated Parmesan cheese

When I lived in Ecuador, my roommate, Sara, was forever receiving care packages from her mother in Spain, with delicacies like chorizo and saffron. So when she announced she wanted to make traditional paella, I jumped at the opportunity to help. We used the crumbling chimney on our rooftop to build a makeshift fire, over which we set bomba rice, chorizo, prawns, and spices to simmer in a two-foot-wide cast-iron pan. This camping-friendly version is quicker, using the more commonly found Arborio rice and cured salami. Hold back from stirring the rice while it cooks; this will prevent the starch from being released and preserve the individual grains like a true paella. If you prefer, substitute 1 cup frozen peas for the sugar snap peas and add them with the salami. I like to use large shrimp with the tail intact so they're easy to pluck out of the paella. You can prepare this over the camp stove or, more traditionally, over the campfire. It's easy and impressive.

---

1   Fire the grill or campfire to medium-high heat and position the grill grate 4 inches above the coals.

2   In a 12-inch cast-iron skillet or deep, lidded saucepan over medium heat, warm 1 tablespoon of the olive oil (direct heat if cooking over a campfire). Add the peas and ¼ teaspoon of the salt, toss the peas to coat with oil, and cook, stirring often, until browned and tender, 5 to 6 minutes. Once cooked, transfer the peas to a bowl and set aside.

3   Add 1 tablespoon olive oil and the onion to the pan, toss to coat, and sauté until translucent and soft, about 5 minutes. Add the garlic, salami, rice, mushrooms (if using), and remaining 1 tablespoon olive oil and stir until the rice is coated with oil. Add the smoked paprika, turmeric, saffron (if using), chicken broth, tomatoes, and remaining ¼ teaspoon salt to the pan and mix together until combined. Using the back of a stirring spoon, spread the rice mixture into an even layer in the pan.

4   Bring to a boil, then lower to a simmer, cover, and cook until the rice has absorbed all the liquid, about 25 minutes. (Do not stir! That will release the starch in the rice and create a gooier consistency. You can peek quickly to check for doneness.) After 25 minutes, remove the lid.

5   Stir in the cooked snap peas, lemon zest, and olives (if using). One by one, add the shrimp, pushing them so that they're buried in the rice. Cover the pan and cook until the shrimp are pink and cooked through, about 5 minutes. Remove the paella from the heat (take extra caution to protect your hands with welding gloves as the pan will be scorching hot) and let stand, covered, for 10 minutes to cool. Sprinkle the parsley and Parmesan over top.

6   Serve warm directly from the pan. (Be sure to warn your fellow campers that the pan is hot!) Store leftovers in an airtight container, chilled, for up to 3 days.

Note: Before being sliced, a salami log can last up to six weeks at room temperature. If you're using some for dinner at camp, and the temperature dips overnight, you can still add leftovers to your breakfast the next morning. For this dish, the best salami choices are Genoa, soppressata, or Spanish-style chorizo.

main events

Every year in Mecklenburg, New York, local iron welder and artist Durand Van Doren hosts a Midwinter Pie Potluck at his forge. Outside, giant bonfires bathe snow-covered fields with light, and smaller conversational fire circles hold savory surprises: grilled cheeses, foil-packet roasted garlic, and Mark Sarvary's legendary Hungarian goulash. Inspired by his recipe, this version combines elements of Italian minestrone and classic American chili. It also takes after Mark's philosophy that if you're making stew, you might as well make enough for a crowd. (You can freeze it in an airtight container for up to 6 months.) Since braising meat requires more cooking time (and fuel), add an extra propane canister to your packing list.

To make this vegan, substitute 6 tablespoons olive oil for the butter, 1 pound stemmed and sliced shiitake mushrooms for the beef, and vegetable broth instead of beef broth.

---

**PREP** In a ziplock bag, combine the beef, sweet paprika, smoked paprika, garlic, salt, and pepper. Seal the bag, use your hands to evenly coat the beef with the seasonings, and then chill for up to 24 hours.

1   In an 8-quart Dutch oven over medium heat, melt the butter. Once the butter begins to foam (before it browns!), add the onions, stir to coat with the butter, cover, and cook until translucent and soft, about 5 minutes.

2   Add the beef and all of its seasonings to the pot, turn the heat to medium, and cook, stirring occasionally, until the beef is browned and coated in a creamy sauce, about 5 minutes. The pan may seem too dry, but as the beef breaks down it will release fat. Add the bell peppers, potatoes, carrots, bay leaves, and beans to the beef and stir to combine. Stir in the tomatoes and their juice, breaking them up with a spoon, then pour in the beef broth. Bring to a boil, then lower to a simmer and cook until the beef is tender, about 45 minutes. Stir in the cornmeal and cook until the chili thickens, about 5 minutes.

3   Ladle the chili directly into each camper's bowl, topping with a dollop of the yogurt and a sprinkle of parsley.

4   Serve immediately. Store leftovers in an airtight container, chilled, for up to 4 days.

# ZERO-DEGREE CHILI

PREP: 25 minutes
COOK: 60 minutes
YIELD: 8 to 10 servings

---

1½ pounds beef stew meat (see Note), cut into ½-inch pieces

¼ cup sweet paprika

1 tablespoon smoked paprika

1 tablespoon minced garlic

2 teaspoons kosher salt

20 turns of the pepper mill

3 tablespoons unsalted butter

1⅔ cups diced onions

2 bell peppers, seeded and diced

2 cups chopped potatoes (½-inch pieces)

2 medium carrots, diced

2 bay leaves

One 15-ounce can kidney beans, drained and rinsed

One 28-ounce can whole peeled tomatoes

4 cups beef broth

¼ cup cornmeal

½ cup plain yogurt or sour cream

Finely chopped fresh parsley or cilantro for garnish

Note: If there's fat on the beef, keep it for flavor!

Pasta has always been one of my favorite one-pan camping dinners, but there was the nuisance of draining and evenly distributing all that scorching hot water in the woods. When I discovered that you could cook pasta right in its own sauce, without first boiling it in water and then adding sauce, I was hooked. What's more, the results are nearly always better! The starch released from the pasta creates a luscious, creamy sauce that coats every noodle, elbow, and penne. And, of course, there are fewer dishes to clean up, a camping win!

# one-pan pastas

# BANH MI PAD THAI NOODLES

PREP: 10 minutes

COOK: 12 minutes

YIELD: 4 servings

### VIETNAMESE PEANUT SAUCE

¼ cup coconut milk (see Note, page 172), stirred

¼ cup creamy peanut butter

2 tablespoons freshly squeezed lime juice

1 teaspoon honey

½ teaspoon kosher salt

½ teaspoon grated garlic

¼ teaspoon peeled, grated ginger

¼ teaspoon red pepper flakes, or to taste

8 ounces uncooked stir-fry rice noodles (aka rice or pad thai noodles)

1 cup dried mushroom pieces, any variety

2 cups water, plus 1 to 2 tablespoons

2 tablespoons toasted sesame oil

1 teaspoon kosher salt

1 cup assorted Quick Pickles (page 38), coarsely chopped

1 cup loosely packed fresh cilantro leaves

½ cup unsalted roasted peanuts, coarsely chopped

½ cup mung bean sprouts

This recipe combines two of my favorite dishes, pad thai noodles and Vietnamese banh mi sandwiches. Once you take a bite, you won't be able to stop. Every forkful holds a new surprise—crunchy peanuts, fresh sprouts, bright herbs, and tangy colorful pickles—all held together by a luxurious peanut sauce. I learned how to make a variation of this sauce at the Red Bridge Cooking School in Vietnam. Our outdoor kitchen overlooked the Thu Bồn River, with simple stations for each student: one cutting board, one knife, one camp stove, one pan, one pot, and a stirring spoon. Several weeks later in Ho Chi Minh City, I had my first banh mi sandwich, and the idea for this mash-up was born. While not authentic, this dish will introduce you to some of the key flavors in Southeast Asian cuisine, re-created with ingredients available in the United States. This is great served as a cold pasta salad for lunch. Double the peanut sauce recipe to have extra on hand as a dip for raw vegetables or add to a tortilla wrap with tofu, quick pickles, cilantro, and bean sprouts.

PREP To make the peanut sauce: In a blender, combine the coconut milk, peanut butter, lime juice, honey, salt, garlic, ginger, and red pepper flakes. Whiz until smooth and creamy, about 1 minute. Transfer to an airtight container and store, chilled, for up to 3 weeks.

1  Remove the peanut sauce from the cooler about 30 minutes before cooking to bring to ambient temperature. If it's cold, it may need up to 1 hour to soften.

2  In a 12-inch cast-iron skillet over high heat, combine the noodles, mushrooms, 2 cups water, sesame oil, and salt. Bring to a boil, then lower to a simmer and cook until the noodles are al dente, 10 to 12 minutes. Using tongs, mix every few minutes to prevent the noodles from sticking to the pan. Add the peanut sauce and 1 to 2 tablespoons water to the pan and mix until the noodles are evenly coated. Stir in the pickles and evenly sprinkle the cilantro, peanuts, and mung bean sprouts over the top.

3  Serve warm directly from the pan. Store leftovers in an airtight container, chilled, for up to 5 days.

# MARINARA PASTA BAKE WITH TUNA AND CAPERS

I was ecstatic to discover that this childhood favorite, traditionally baked in the oven, was faster to prepare and just as good on the stove top. While making your own marinara sauce is easy and rewarding, you can substitute store-bought in a pinch. If you're using capers packed in salt, rinse them first.

PREP: 5 minutes

COOK: 11 minutes

YIELD: 6 servings

---

4⅔ cups penne

1½ cups Homemade Marinara Sauce (facing page)

1½ cups water

2 tablespoons olive oil

One 3½-ounce jar capers, drained

Two 6-ounce tuna foil packets (see Note), drained

2 cups shredded mozzarella cheese

Red pepper flakes for sprinkling (optional)

1   In a 12-inch cast-iron skillet over high heat, combine the penne, ½ cup of the marinara sauce, the water, and olive oil and stir together with a wooden spoon. Bring to a boil, then lower to a simmer and cook until the pasta is al dente, about 11 minutes.

2   Remove from the heat and stir in the remaining 1 cup marinara sauce, the capers, and drained tuna, breaking up and evenly distributing the tuna with a wooden spoon. Add the mozzarella and stir until the cheese melts.

3   Serve warm directly from the pan, sprinkled with red pepper flakes, if desired. Store leftovers in an airtight container, chilled, for up to 3 days.

Note: Tuna pouches are perfect for camping—lightweight, easily packed, and shelf-stable. The Monterey Bay Aquarium's Seafood Watch is a user-friendly online guide to help consumers make choices in support of a healthy ocean. For tuna, they recommend troll-or pole-caught albacore and skipjack. Visit www.seafoodwatch.org for good alternatives.

This homemade sauce is great for dipping your crusts from Grilled Hawaiian Pizza (page 140) or dunking Charred Bread (page 102), or double the recipe and freeze extra for quick pasta nights or last-minute camping trips. (Frozen sauce also doubles as cooler ice.) My favorite Italian brand of strained tomatoes is Pomi; it's widely available in supermarkets and contains *just* tomatoes. Feel free to add a splash of red wine for a richer sauce. I prefer to whiz the marinara sauce in a blender until smooth, but it's equally good chunky.

# HOMEMADE MARINARA SAUCE

PREP: 15 minutes
COOK: 10 minutes
YIELD: 2 cups

---

3 tablespoons olive oil

1 cup finely chopped yellow onion

½ cup finely chopped carrots

1 tablespoon grated garlic

2 cups strained tomatoes
(such as Pomi)

½ teaspoon kosher salt

20 turns of the pepper mill

¼ cup loosely packed, chopped fresh basil leaves, or 1 tablespoon dried basil or pesto

1 tablespoon chopped fresh oregano leaves, or 2 teaspoons dried

1 tablespoon minced fresh rosemary, or 1 tablespoon dried, crushed with your fingers

1½ teaspoons fresh thyme leaves, or 1 teaspoon dried

1   In a medium saucepan over low heat, warm the olive oil. Add the onion, turn the heat to medium, and sauté until translucent and soft, 5 to 7 minutes. Add the carrots and garlic and sauté until the garlic begins to brown, 3 to 5 minutes.

2   Stir the tomatoes, salt, and pepper into the pan. Cover and simmer until the carrots are fork-tender, 10 to 15 minutes. Stir in the basil, oregano, rosemary, and thyme and simmer for 2 minutes, uncovered, to allow the herbs to infuse the sauce; adding the herbs last keeps their flavors fresh and bright. Remove from the heat and let cool.

3   Store in an airtight container, chilled, for up to 1 week, or freeze for up to 6 months.

# BURNT BROCCOLI MAC 'N' CHEESE

PREP: 15 minutes

COOK: 40 minutes

YIELD: 4 servings

---

1 head broccoli

4 tablespoons olive oil

1 cup water

½ cup whole milk

1 teaspoon kosher salt

2 tablespoons unsalted butter

1 large onion, very thinly sliced

2 cups elbow macaroni

3 cups shredded cheddar cheese

1 teaspoon mustard powder

20 turns of the pepper mill

Red pepper flakes for sprinkling (optional)

Are your friends gathered with you around the campfire? Good. Because you'll want company to share this bowl of soul food. For omnivores, finish the dish with crispy bacon bits or flecks of candied, smoked salmon. If preparing at home, you can freeze for up to 2 months and reheat, uncovered, in a 375°F oven until warmed through, about 1 hour.

---

**PREP** Slice the broccoli head lengthwise into 1-inch-thick "steaks." Put the broccoli and 2 tablespoons of the olive oil in a ziplock bag. Seal the bag, use your hands to evenly coat the broccoli with the oil, and then chill for up to 2 days.

In a large lidded jar, combine the water, milk, remaining 2 tablespoons olive oil, and ½ teaspoon of the salt. Seal the jar tightly, shake vigorously until incorporated, and then chill for up to 2 days.

1   Fire the grill to medium-high heat and position the grill grate 4 inches above the coals.

2   Using tongs, place the broccoli "steaks" over direct heat and cook until evenly charred and tender, 5 to 7 minutes per side. To prevent burning, transfer to indirect heat to finish cooking until tender. When done, transfer to a plate or cutting board, let cool slightly, and cut into bite-size pieces. Set aside.

3   On a camp stove, in a 12-inch cast-iron skillet or sauté pan over medium-low heat, melt 1 tablespoon of the butter. Add the onion and use tongs to coat with the butter. Turn the heat to medium and cook until the onion is caramel brown, about 15 minutes, or longer for darker color. Stir occasionally to prevent burning. If the onion begins to burn, turn the heat to medium-low.

4   Stir the broccoli, macaroni, and milk mixture into the onion. Bring to a boil, then lower to a simmer, cover, and cook until al dente, 7 to 9 minutes, stirring halfway through cooking to prevent the pasta from sticking to the pan. Remove the pan from the heat.

5   Add the cheddar, mustard powder, pepper, remaining 1 tablespoon butter, and remaining ½ teaspoon salt and stir until the cheese and butter are melted.

6   Serve warm directly from the pan. Set out red pepper flakes so campers can sprinkle directly over their mac 'n' cheese as desired. Store leftovers in an airtight container, chilled, for up to 5 days.

On the morning of my first family fishing trip in the Italian Dolomites, my uncle took my twin sister and me with him on a ten-mile bike ride to the mountain lake while the rest of the family went by car. We straggled in at the end of the day, with him carrying our bikes over his shoulder. My mom was so relieved to see us! We had been so excited to fish that she helped us cast a few lines right away, and we each caught a trout to add to the cooler my little siblings had nearly filled. Back at the cabin, my mom cleaned and then seared the fish in a skillet with olive oil, serving them alongside a giant bowl of spaghetti. We were young but because we helped catch the fish we could all recognize that the trout were both a sacrifice and a gift to our table.

Although not a common practice in the United States, eating fish whole is widely enjoyed around the world. A whole fish is half the price of prepared fillets and more flavorful. The "cheek" of the fish is especially silky and tender, and not to be missed! When buying whole fish, ask your fishmonger to scale and clean it for you. Before serving, either consult an article or video on "how to fillet (or carve) and serve whole fish" or prepare to pick at the fish with a fork, dodging the bones.

---

**PREP** Pat the fish dry from head to tail with paper towels. Using your hands, coat each side with 1½ teaspoons of the olive oil and ½ teaspoon salt. Sprinkle both sides with the pepper.

Insert the lemon slices and parsley into the cavity of the fish and sprinkle with a pinch of salt. Place the fish in a ziplock bag. To prevent the lemons and parsley from falling out of the cavity, wrap the bag around the fish and hold it in place with a rubber band or masking tape and then chill for up to 24 hours.

Wash the radishes and greens in a colander to remove any grit and then pat dry with a tea towel. In a ziplock bag, combine the radishes, garlic, ¼ cup olive oil, and ½ teaspoon salt. Seal the bag, use your hands to evenly coat the radishes and greens with the oil, and then chill for 24 hours.

continued

# PAN-SEARED RAINBOW TROUT WITH WHOLE RADISHES

**PREP:** 5 minutes
**COOK:** 7 minutes
**YIELD:** 2 servings

---

**One 10- to 12-ounce whole rainbow or other trout, scaled and cleaned**

**¼ cup plus 2 tablespoons olive oil**

**Kosher salt**

**10 turns of the pepper mill**

**1 lemon, thinly sliced**

**1 tablespoon finely chopped fresh parsley**

**8 to 10 radishes with greens attached (see Note)**

**2 large garlic cloves, thinly sliced lengthwise**

Note: Look for radishes with healthy, lush greens. The greens, too often tossed away, are rich in nutrition and earthy and sweet like the roots when cooked.

1   In a 12-inch cast-iron skillet over medium heat, warm the remaining 1 tablespoon olive oil. When the oil is hot, place the trout in the center of the pan. (If the trout is too long for the pan, you can bend it to fit or cut off the tail section and place it alongside the body.) Arrange the radishes, their greens, and garlic around the edges, tossing to coat with the oil. Cook the fish, while tossing the radishes frequently with tongs, until the first side is brown and crispy, about 2 minutes. The radish leaves will begin to char, the radishes will pale in color, and the garlic will begin to brown. Use a metal spatula to flip the fish, being sure to scrape from the bottom of the pan so the crispy skin stays intact!

2   Cook until the other side is brown and crispy, about 2 minutes more, then flip the fish again and turn off the heat. Let the fish rest in the hot pan for 3 minutes more and continue tossing the radishes. Use a thermometer to check that the internal temperature of the thickest part of the flesh is 140°F, or that the flesh easily flakes apart with a fork.

3   Serve warm directly from the pan (be sure to warn your fellow campers that the pan is hot!) or transfer to a cutting board to carve the fish. Store leftovers in an airtight container or ziplock bag, chilled, for up to 3 days.

No matter the weather or size of the crowd, Aunt JoAnne serves this year after year on December 23. And every year, I bundle up and follow her out to the driveway to watch the salmon smolder on the charcoal grill. It's an incredibly simple recipe, but the result is magnificent: juicy, perfectly seasoned, and infused with the primal taste of smoke. After Bobby and I realized we spent the remaining 364 days of the year anticipating this dish, we tracked down our own bag of alder-wood chips at the local hardware store so we could make this dish whenever we craved it. This recipe requires a grill with a lid and alder-wood chips, so plan on bringing these when you're making this at the campground. Leftovers are delicious scrambled with eggs.

---

**PREP** In a small lidded jar, combine the olive oil, garlic, oregano, salt, and pepper. Shake vigorously until incorporated and then chill for up to 3 days.

1   Submerge 1½ cups alder-wood chips in a bowl of water and soak for 30 minutes before cooking.

2   Fire the grill to medium heat and position the grill grate 4 inches above the coals. Line a baking sheet with parchment paper or aluminum foil.

3   Pat the salmon dry with paper towels and place on the prepared baking sheet. Drizzle the olive oil mixture over the top, using a pastry brush or the back of a spoon to coat the fillet. Sprinkle the paprika evenly over the top.

4   Place the wood chips on the hot coals. When the wood chips start smoking, transfer the salmon to the grill over direct heat and remove and recycle the parchment paper or aluminum foil, leaving a clean baking sheet. Close the lid and cook until the salmon is firm and easily flakes apart with a fork, 8 to 10 minutes, or use a thermometer to check that the internal temperature has reached 140°F. (If you see white juice seeping out—a protein called albumin—it's overcooked. But don't worry, drizzling additional oil over the whole fillet will moisten it.) Transfer the salmon to the baking sheet and let rest for 5 minutes, then slice the whole fillet into portions.

5   Serve directly from the baking sheet with lemon wedges for campers to squeeze over top. Store leftovers in an airtight container, chilled, for up to 3 days.

# JOANNE'S ALDER WOOD-SMOKED SALMON

PREP: 5 minutes
COOK: 8 to 10 minutes
YIELD: 4 to 6 servings

---

**2 tablespoons olive oil, plus more for drizzling**

**1 tablespoon minced garlic**

**1 teaspoon chopped fresh oregano leaves, or ½ teaspoon dried**

**1 teaspoon kosher salt**

**20 turns of the pepper mill**

**1½ pounds whole wild salmon fillet with skin (see Note)**

**½ teaspoon paprika**

**1 lemon, cut into wedges**

Note: My favorite salmon for this dish is bright crimson, flavorful sockeye, which you can buy direct from Wild For Salmon and keep on hand in the freezer until ready to use.

main events

Foil packets are one of the best—and easiest—ways to prepare juicy, flavorful salmon. I created this recipe with Coley Gaffney, my cast mate on *Food Network Star*, as part of a multicourse "dinner and a movie" event at Firelight Camps. We paired this dish with a documentary about wild salmon—*The Breach*—projected on the canvas of our lobby tent. In this dish, tart blueberries and honey are muddled together to create a violet-colored sauce that elevates the toothsome wild salmon. You can also substitute a spoonful of Basil–Sunflower Seed Pesto (page 80) or Mamma's Salsa Verde (see page 167) for the blueberry sauce.

**PREP** In a lidded jar, combine the blueberries, honey, and lemon juice. Use the back of a spoon to gently smash and muddle the blueberries with the honey and lemon juice. Seal the jar tightly and then chill for up to 3 days.

Put four 12-inch-square sheets of aluminum foil on a work surface. Lay 3 lemon slices, with edges overlapping like dominoes, in the center of each foil sheet and top with a frozen salmon fillet. Season the salmon with the salt and lightly dust with pepper. Top each salmon fillet with 2 thyme sprigs.

Fold up two sides of the foil to meet in the middle and fold the edges over each other to seal the top. Then fold the two open ends of the foil to seal the packet. Seal the salmon packets in a ziplock bag and then chill for up to 24 hours.

1   Fire the grill to medium heat and position the grill grate 4 inches above the coals.

2   Using tongs, place the foil packets over direct heat and cook for 8 minutes. Using two forks, open the foil seal along the top, allowing the steam to escape and preventing the salmon from overcooking. Use a thermometer to check that the internal temperature has reached 140°F. An easier way to check for doneness is with a fork; the salmon should be firm and easily flake apart. (If you see white juice seeping out—a protein called albumin—it's overcooked. But don't worry, the blueberry syrup will moisten the fillet.)

3   Serve the salmon directly from the foil—fewer plates to clean!—and spoon the blueberries over the top. Store leftovers in an airtight container, chilled, for up to 1 day.

# FOIL-PACKET SALMON WITH LEMON, THYME, AND BLUEBERRY

 GF

PREP: 5 minutes
COOK: 8 minutes
YIELD: 4 servings

¼ cup fresh or frozen blueberries

2 teaspoons honey

1 tablespoon freshly squeezed lemon juice, plus 2 lemons, each cut into 6 thin slices

Four 6-ounce wild salmon fillets, frozen (see Note)

2 teaspoons kosher salt

Freshly ground black pepper

8 thyme sprigs

Note: Frozen seafood is often-times fresher than "fresh" seafood. When handled properly, it has been frozen within hours of harvest, preserving both the quality and flavor of the fish at its peak. Ask your fishmonger where the seafood is from and when it was harvested, or purchase directly from an online buying club such as Wild for Salmon, Alaska Gold, and Vital Choice. Your freezer will be stocked with last-minute meals!

main events

# CRISPY LEMON-THYME SKILLET CHICKEN WITH GREEN BEANS

PREP: 10 minutes
COOK: 15 to 20 minutes
YIELD: 2 to 4 servings

---

2 boneless chicken breasts

2 lemons

1 teaspoon kosher salt

20 turns of the pepper mill

2½ tablespoons unsalted butter

8 ounces green beans

4 or 5 thyme sprigs

This dish proves that with a few key, fresh ingredients you can create a masterpiece. Thyme and lemon are a bewitching combination, more so when combined with butter. This simple seasoning is all that's needed to make a decadent dish in the woods. Engage your senses as you watch for even charring on the beans and listen for the hiss of the chicken hitting the buttered pan, key to creating a crispy skin—you'll want that skin on your chicken when you're buying it! Use any leftover chicken for quesadillas, pizza (see page 140), or extra protein in Carol's Favorite Pasta Salad with Tomatoes, Basil, and Mozzarella (page 88).

---

**PREP** Cover the chicken breasts with plastic wrap and pound with a mallet or the bottom of a glass jar or bottle until they are 1 inch thick; this will help them cook more quickly and evenly.

Finely grate the zest of the lemons and set aside. Reserve the lemons in a ziplock bag and then chill for up to 1 week; you can use them to squeeze lemon juice over the chicken at camp.

In a small bowl, use a fork or your fingers to mix together the lemon zest, salt, and pepper and rub it evenly on both sides of the chicken breasts. Store in an airtight container or ziplock bag, chilled, for up to 24 hours.

1   In a 12-inch cast-iron skillet or frying pan over medium-low heat, melt the butter. Once the butter begins to foam (before it browns!), use tongs to place the chicken breasts in the middle of the pan—they will hiss as they begin to sear. Using tongs, scatter the green beans around the edges of the pan and toss with the butter. Scatter the thyme sprigs in the pan, then toss the beans frequently, until they are wrinkled and charred.

2   Cook the chicken until the first side is brown and crispy, 3 to 5 minutes. Flip the chicken and continue to cook until the other side is brown and crispy, 3 to 5 minutes more. Move the chicken to the edge of the pan to continue cooking until done, another 10 minutes. Use a thermometer to confirm the internal temperature of the thickest section of the breast has reached 165°F, or slice the breast in half and make sure there is no pink flesh. If the beans finish

cooking before the chicken, pile them on top of the chicken breasts to prevent them from charring further, or transfer them to a separate bowl or plate.

3   Transfer the skillet to a heatproof surface or trivet. If you've removed the beans, scatter them back around the chicken. Cut the lemons into wedges and squeeze lemon juice over the top.

4   Serve warm directly from the skillet. (Be sure to warn your fellow campers that the skillet is hot!) Store leftovers in an airtight container, chilled, for up to 4 days.

I love coriander, but it wasn't until I made this recipe that I discovered how beautifully it pairs with honey and paprika, so much so that the Roasted Corn Salsa carries the same pairing and enriches the overall dish. This glaze is superb on meats as well as grilled vegetables or brushed on toast with butter. This is an endless-summer recipe, perfect for the short, miraculous window when corn, herbs, and tomatoes can all be found growing in the fields. You can also re-create this recipe in winter, using frozen sweet corn and cooking the pork chops under the broiler.

---

**PREP** In a small bowl, whisk together the honey, olive oil, vinegar, coriander seeds, salt, paprika, garlic, and pepper to form a glaze. Transfer 2 tablespoons of the glaze to a small lidded jar or airtight container and then chill for up to 3 days.

In a ziplock bag, combine the remaining glaze with the pork chops. Seal the bag, use your hands to coat the pork chops, and then chill for up to 24 hours.

1   Fire the grill to high heat, create a two-zone fire (see page 27), and position the grill grate 4 inches from the coals.

2   Place the pork chops over direct heat and grill until charred, 2 to 3 minutes on each side. Let the flames lick the meat! Transfer the pork chops to the edge of the direct heat zone and continue to cook until the pork chops are firm to the touch, 5 to 7 minutes on each side. Use a thermometer to check that the internal temperature of the thickest section of the pork chops is 145°F. An easier way to check for doneness is to cut through the thickest part of the pork chop; the inside should be light brown, not pink. Let the meat rest for 10 minutes to allow the juices to redistribute.

3   Serve the pork chops on a cutting board or serving plate, or transfer to campers' plates. With the back of a spoon, spread the 2 tablespoons glaze evenly over the pork chops. Top each serving with a heaping spoonful of salsa. Store leftovers in an airtight container, chilled, for up to 4 days.

# HONEY-CORIANDER GLAZED PORK CHOPS WITH ROASTED CORN SALSA

PREP: 10 minutes

COOK: 18 minutes

YIELD: 4 to 6 servings

---

¼ cup honey

2 tablespoons olive oil

2 teaspoons apple cider vinegar

1 tablespoon toasted coriander seeds, crushed

1½ teaspoons kosher salt

1 teaspoon sweet paprika

1 teaspoon grated garlic

20 turns of the pepper mill

6 thick pork chops

1 cup Roasted Corn Salsa (page 107)

# RHUBARB-ECUE COUNTRY RIBS

PREP: 10 minutes
COOK: 60 minutes
YIELD: 8 servings

---

2 pounds rhubarb stalks, cut into 1-inch pieces

½ cup maple syrup

¼ cup molasses

1 teaspoon peeled, finely grated fresh ginger

1½ tablespoons olive oil

1 cup chopped red or yellow onion

2 teaspoons minced garlic

1 teaspoon kosher salt

1 teaspoon freshly ground black pepper

½ cup tomato puree

2 teaspoons mustard seeds

¼ teaspoon ground cinnamon

¼ teaspoon smoked paprika

⅛ teaspoon ground cloves

1 teaspoon Chinese dark soy sauce or tamari

2 pounds country-style pork ribs

Rhubarb is a fleeting, late-spring crop that always marks the start of summer. While its humongous leaves are poisonous, the red-and-green-streaked stalks are harvested and most often used for baked goods. When cooked down, they turn from tart and mouth-puckering to sweet and tangy. Preserving those same elements, this "rhubarbecue" sauce transforms grilled ribs, making a succulent, savory dish with this spring gem. This is a primal, messy finger food, so it's best to tuck a napkin in your shirt collar and just dig in, gnawing the meat straight off the bone. Serve with Charred Bread (page 102) or grilled polenta (see page 143) to mop up extra sauce. With a well-stocked pantry, the only ingredients you will need to pick up are rhubarb, ribs, and Chinese dark soy sauce, which is thicker and sweeter than Japanese dark soy sauce (often labeled "all-purpose soy sauce") and adds more depth.

---

PREP In a large pot over high heat, combine the rhubarb, maple syrup, molasses, and ginger. Bring to a boil, then lower to a simmer, cover, and cook until the rhubarb begins to dissolve into a stringy texture, about 7 minutes.

Meanwhile, in a small pot over medium-low heat, warm the olive oil. Add the onion, turn the heat to medium, and sauté until translucent and soft, about 5 minutes. Add the garlic, salt, and pepper and stir until the onion and garlic begin to brown, 3 to 5 minutes. Stir in the tomato puree, cover, and simmer to let the flavors combine for 2 to 3 minutes.

Pour the tomato mixture into the rhubarb and add the mustard seeds, cinnamon, paprika, cloves, and soy sauce. Stir thoroughly and continue to simmer, uncovered, until the sauce reduces by half, about 20 minutes. Remove from the heat and let cool.

Transfer ¼ cup of the rhubarbecue sauce to an airtight container and then chill for up to 1 week.

Combine the ribs and remaining rhubarbecue sauce in a ziplock bag. Seal the bag, use your hands to evenly coat the ribs with the sauce, and then chill for up to 3 days.

1   Fire the grill to medium-high heat and position the grill grate 4 inches above the coals. Remove the ribs from the cooler about 10 minutes before you plan to cook them.

2   Remove the ribs from the ziplock bag with tongs, leaving them coated with as much sauce as possible, and place over direct heat. Discard the remaining marinade. Cook the ribs until caramelized and browned, 6 to 10 minutes on each side. Use a thermometer to check that the internal temperature of the thickest rib is 145°F or higher. An easier way to check for doneness is to cut through the thickest rib; the inside should be light brown, not pink. Let rest for 10 minutes.

3   The ribs will be tender, juicy, and intact, and are best eaten directly off the bone. Serve the rhubarbecue sauce alongside so each camper can spoon on as desired. Store leftovers in an airtight container, chilled, for up to 3 days.

In January 1985, when my mother was consulting for several Italian wineries from our home in Denver, she was featured as *Bon Appétit* magazine's "great cook" of the month. The food editor was a good friend, and upon sharing with my mother that it was difficult to find accomplished home cooks for this section, Mamma volunteered with enthusiasm; she was already known for her dinner parties. The resulting seven-page spread featured eight original Italian recipes that showcased her roots, noting that, "Almost everything is made ahead of time because she wants to enjoy her own party." Not to mention she had twin daughters not yet a year old at that point and was also working full time. When I'm camping, I also want to relax at dinner, which is why I love this easy, bright sauce with high-voltage flavor (it's been passed down for generations in our family). It's the perfect complement to nearly any entrée or side dish, especially skirt steak. The affordable cut cooks fast on the grill, yielding a crispy crust and juicy interior. Leftover steak can be used for sandwich, taco, and quesadilla fillings. Keep extra salsa on hand for spreading on Charred Bread (page 102), or spooning over coal-baked potatoes (see page 123), eggs, and fish. If you're using capers packed in salt, rinse them first.

---

**PREP** To prepare the salsa verde: In a food processor, combine the garlic, anchovies, and capers and pulse until finely chopped. Scrape down the sides of the processor bowl; add the vinegar, mustard, and parsley; and whiz while slowly drizzling in the ⅓ cup olive oil until smooth and bright green. Transfer the mixture to a lidded 8-ounce jar. Add the remaining 1 tablespoon olive oil over the top to create a film that will preserve the lovely bright green. Seal the jar tightly and chill for up to 1 week.

Dry-brine the steaks by rubbing the salt evenly over the surface. (You can also do this 1 to 2 hours before cooking at camp.) Transfer to a ziplock bag and then chill for up to 24 hours.

1   Remove the salsa verde from the cooler and let stand at ambient temperature for up to 2 hours before serving.

2   Fire the grill to high heat and position the grill grate as close as possible to the coals or pile the coals high under

continued

# FIRE-LICKED SKIRT STEAK WITH MAMMA'S SALSA VERDE

PREP: 10 minutes
COOK: 10 to 12 minutes
YIELD: 4 to 6 servings

**MAMMA'S SALSA VERDE**

1 large or 2 small garlic cloves, peeled

One 2-ounce can anchovy fillets, rinsed and patted dry

2 tablespoons capers

1 teaspoon red wine vinegar or sherry vinegar

½ teaspoon Dijon mustard

½ cup coarsely chopped fresh parsley

⅓ cup olive oil, plus 1 tablespoon

2 pounds skirt steak (see Note)

2 teaspoons kosher salt

20 turns of the pepper mill

Note: Some recipes suggest trimming the steak's fat to prevent flare-ups when the fat drips onto the coals. Skirt steak isn't very fatty, but still, leave any fat on for flavor and just be prepared for flare-ups (see "How to Squelch a Grease Fire," page 26).

main events

the grate to maximize the steak's proximity to the fire. Remove the steaks from the cooler and pat dry with a paper towel to eliminate moisture on the surface and ensure a crispy crust. Sprinkle both sides with the pepper.

3   Place the steaks over the hottest part of the fire. Using long tongs, flip the steak every minute or so for even cooking; the cooking time will vary depending on thickness.

4   Look for an evenly caramelized and browned outer crust to check doneness. Slight char is okay but don't let the crust burn! Use a thermometer to check that the internal temperature of the thickest part of the steak is between 125° and 130°F for medium-rare to medium. You can cook longer for medium-well or well-done, though it will make the steak chewier.

5   Transfer the steak to a cutting board and let rest for 10 minutes so the juices can redistribute. Slice the steak *against* the grain into ½-inch slices.

6   Serve directly from the cutting board. Stir the top layer of oil into the salsa verde just before serving and let campers add it to their steak directly from the jar. Store leftovers in an airtight container, chilled, for up to 3 days.

# SWEET
# ENDINGS

While almost every American dish has foreign origins, the s'more is a true American creation and the quintessential campfire treat. In this section, I offer variations on more camping classics as well as some new ideas to complete your feast by firelight.

# STRAWBERRY GINGERSNAP CHIA SEED PUDDING

PREP: 5 minutes

CHILL: 30 to 60 minutes

YIELD: 2 servings

---

5 large strawberries, stemmed and sliced

1 cup coconut milk (see Note)

1 tablespoon honey

½ teaspoon vanilla extract

Finely grated zest and juice of 1 lemon

2 tablespoons chia seeds

2 tablespoons crushed gingersnap cookies

Chia seed pudding is the new Jell-O. When soaked in liquid, the seeds swell and release a powerful dose of nutrients, including fiber, antioxidants, omega-3 fats, proteins, vitamins, and minerals. This was common practice during the time of the ancient Aztecs, who relied on chia seeds as a major crop, a form of payment, and a sacred medicinal food and beverage that was said to provide enough energy for a full day trekking through the desert. Today, chia seeds power outdoor warriors like us. The proof is in the pudding, literally. My favorite way to use this superfood, hardly bigger than a poppy seed, is to make a creamy and wholesome dessert that is camp-friendly. It's fair game for breakfast, too, especially when topped with Firelight Quinoa Granola Clusters (page 40). Feel free to use other berries of your choice.

---

**PREP** In a blender, combine one-third of the strawberries, the coconut milk, honey, vanilla, and 1 tablespoon of the lemon juice and whiz until smooth. Store in a lidded jar or airtight container, chilled, for up to 2 days.

Pack the remaining strawberry slices in an airtight container, chilled, for up to 2 days.

1   Transfer the strawberry mixture to a medium bowl or airtight container. Stir in the chia seeds and another one-third of the strawberry slices. Scatter the remaining strawberry slices and the lemon zest over the top.

2   Cover the bowl with plastic wrap or seal the container and chill for at least 30 minutes, ideally up to 60 minutes. Jiggle the bowl; if the mixture is firm, the pudding is ready.

3   Just before serving, top evenly or artistically with the crushed gingersnaps, then spoon into each camper's bowl. Store leftovers in an airtight container, chilled, for up to 5 days.

Note: Use whole coconut milk, full of good fat and flavor. Light coconut milk has added water.

I first came across fruit fool in the children's book *A Fine Dessert*, which showed the evolution of four families across four centuries, all making the same simple treat. It put a name to the whipped berry puddings my mother always made in the height of summer. One of the oldest recipes in Western culture, a fool is, at its most basic level, fresh fruit and sugar folded into whipped cream. I like to jazz it up with elements of an old-fashioned cocktail, one of my favorite campfire drinks and a fitting name for this time-honored dessert. If serving to kiddos, simply leave out the bourbon, but certainly enlist them to help make the whipped cream! One of my favorite camping hacks, whipped cream can be made in 3 minutes flat by shaking heavy whipping cream in a mason jar with a small pebble or marble. A pebble is easy to find on the trail; but be sure to scrub it clean. Top each serving with scraps of graham crackers for extra decadence and a crunchy finish.

---

**PREP** To make the cherries: In a ziplock bag or airtight container, combine the cherries, orange juice, and maple syrup. Shake to mix the liquid and coat the cherries and then chill for at least 30 minutes or up to 24 hours.

1   To make the whipped cream: In a lidded pint mason jar, combine the whipping cream, maple syrup, bourbon, vanilla, orange zest, and salt. Add a clean pebble or marble, tightly seal the jar, and shake vigorously for 3 minutes without stopping, until you can no longer hear the cream glugging in the jar and it forms stiff peaks when a spoon is dunked in and pulled out. (Any longer and you will be on your way to making butter! See Note.)

2   Transfer the whipped cream to a serving bowl; *be sure to remove the pebble or marble.*

3   Using a slotted spoon, transfer the cherries to the bowl (reserving the orange-maple liquid for a refreshing soda with sparkling water or fixing a bourbon cocktail). Fold the cherries into the whipped cream.

4   Serve individual portions in small bowls or mason jars, topping with crumbled graham crackers, if desired. Store leftovers in an airtight container, chilled, for up to 3 days.

# OLD-FASHIONED BOURBON FOOL WITH CHERRIES

PREP: 7 minutes
COOK: None
YIELD: 2 to 4 servings

## CHERRIES

2 cups dark sweet cherries, pitted and halved

Juice of 1 orange

2 tablespoons maple syrup

## WHIPPED CREAM

1 cup heavy whipping cream

1 tablespoon maple syrup

1 tablespoon bourbon

1 teaspoon vanilla extract

1 teaspoon orange zest

1 pinch fine sea salt (preferably pink Himalayan)

2 Honey Graham Crackers, crumbled (page 44; optional)

Note: If you shake the cream for an extra 8 minutes, you'll have maple-bourbon butter! Strain it from the separated liquid and chill in an airtight container to firm up. Lather on Dutch Oven Rosemary–Sea Salt Cornbread (see page 128).

# GRILLED STONE FRUIT WITH BREAD CRUMBLE

PREP: 15 to 20 minutes
COOK: 30 to 35 minutes
YIELD: 6 servings

## BREAD CRUMBLE

4 thick slices stale bread, broken into popcorn-size crumbs (see Note)

4 tablespoons unsalted butter, cut into slices

½ cup firmly packed light brown sugar

¼ cup honey

1 teaspoon finely grated fresh ginger

1 tablespoon freshly squeezed lemon juice

8 whole farm-fresh stone fruit (such as peaches, apricots, nectarines, or plums)

½ cup heavy cream (optional)

Note: Any bread will work for bread crumble, though sourdough is my favorite. If you don't have stale bread lying around, toast fresh bread before breaking into popcorn-size crumbs.

One summer in Venice, Italy, I was chased out of a market stall for prodding a peach. The red-faced owner scolded, "Would I sell fruit that isn't ripe?!" I was mortified and ran to my mom. She explained that you could choose a ripe peach just by looking for slight depressions, often mistaken for bruising, and that stone fruit in general smelled sweet when ripe. You will need perfectly ripe stone fruit for this recipe, which takes the exquisite experience of eating it fresh to new heights when grilled. This recipe is even easier if you want to bypass the honey-ginger syrup, though I wouldn't recommend skipping the bread crumble. My friend Stefan, owner of Wide Awake Bakery in Ithaca, New York, first introduced me to bread crumble. He said it was so good and so different from anything he had ever tried that he had to make a new category for it in his brain. Bread crumble is made from stale, or "aged," bread that's hardened over a couple days; it's broken into small pieces and caramelized with butter and sugar. Not only is it a resourceful way to use bread that's hardened, it has the same addictive quality of popcorn. Drizzle fresh cream over your dessert; just don't faint when you take a bite.

PREP To make the bread crumble: In a 12-inch cast-iron skillet or frying pan over medium heat, toast the bread crumbs, pushing them around with a wooden spoon, until they begin to brown, about 10 minutes. Turn the heat to medium-low, add the butter and brown sugar, and stir until the crumbs are coated in the melted butter and darkening sugar. Be careful not to let them burn, but don't be afraid of a deep, caramel-colored butter—the flavor will get more complex as it cooks. When the crumbs have reached a color you like, anywhere from almond brown to dark caramel, between 12 to 20 minutes, transfer to a bowl. They will be *very* hot. Let cool completely and harden. Store in an airtight container or ziplock bag at room temperature for up to 3 days, chill for up to 1 week, or freeze for up to 3 months.

In a small pot over medium heat, combine the honey and ginger. Cook until the honey turns to a liquid consistency and then simmer for 5 minutes more. Remove from the heat, whisk in the lemon juice, and let cool. Store in a lidded jar, chilled, for up to 1 week.

1. Fire the grill to medium heat and position the grill grate 4 inches above the coals.

2. Slice the fruit into wedges around the vertical circumference, from stem to tail. Twist each half in opposite directions to open. Remove and compost the pit. If a fruit is too ripe to twist, just remove smaller sections at a time, though you'll have to be extra careful when grilling to make sure they don't fall through the grate. Transfer to a large bowl (or even a pot), baking sheet, or plate and toss the fruit with the honey syrup.

3. Using tongs, place the fruit flesh-side down on the grill and cook until the flesh is scored with grill marks and charred, about 5 minutes. Flip and grill on the skin side until charred, about 5 minutes more. The longer you grill the fruit, the softer it will become—decide what you prefer!

4. Distribute the grilled fruit into each camper's bowl, drizzle with heavy cream, if desired, and sprinkle the bread crumble over the top. Eat up! This is too good to keep leftovers.

# APPLE HARVEST CRISP

PREP: 15 minutes
COOK: 35 to 60 minutes
YIELD: 8 servings

## TOPPING

1 cup rolled oats

½ cup medium-ground corn flour

½ cup almond flour

½ cup almonds or walnuts, coarsely chopped

¼ cup packed coconut sugar or dark brown sugar

Zest of 1 lemon

1 tablespoon poppy seeds

⅛ teaspoon fine salt

## FILLING

5 large baking apples, sliced ¼ inch thick

½ cup honey or maple syrup

Juice of 1 lemon

½ teaspoon vanilla extract

1 pinch freshly grated nutmeg

8 tablespoons butter

One 8-ounce carton heavy whipping cream or plain yogurt

Note: To cook at home, bake, uncovered, in a 375°F oven until the topping is toasted brown and crispy, about 35 minutes.

Many of my friends opt for a Blessing Way in place of a traditional baby shower, which places emphases on gifts. Adopted from a Navajo ritual, a Blessing Way offers spiritual empowerment and support for the mother (and in modern times, the father) as she nears birthing and motherhood. My friends, Peaches and Matteo, held theirs around a campfire outside their cabin, where we shared tales of our mothers and grandmothers. One friend brought an apple-cornmeal crisp, exquisitely spiced and toasted. Made with the fall harvest, it was the perfect way to call upon the strength of Mother Nature.

A Dutch oven crisp is simple, but plan ahead so that the coals can burn down to medium heat. Start cooking the crisp when dinner is served; when you've cleared the last plate, dessert will be ready. Choose a variety of baking apples like Granny Smiths, Mutsus, or Honeycrisps, or swap apples for the same quantity of berries or other orchard fruit. This crisp is lightly sweetened and just as good for breakfast.

---

**PREP** To make the topping: In a large ziplock bag, combine the oats, corn flour, almond flour, almonds, coconut sugar, lemon zest, poppy seeds, and salt. Shake to mix and then chill for up to 24 hours.

To make the filling: In a ziplock bag, combine the apples, honey, lemon juice, vanilla, and nutmeg. Seal the bag, use your hands to evenly coat the apples with the other ingredients, and then chill for up to 24 hours.

1   Fire the grill or campfire to medium heat and position the grill grate 4 inches above the coals.

2   In a small saucepan over the coals, melt the butter. Set aside to cool and then drizzle into the ziplock bag with the topping mixture. Shake to combine until evenly moist.

3   Layer the filling in the bottom of a 5-quart Dutch oven and spread evenly with the topping. Cover the Dutch oven with the lid and place on the grill grate over direct heat. Use tongs to cover the lid with an even layer of hot coals, and as the crisp cooks, add more coals as needed to keep the temperature at medium heat.

4   Cook the crisp until the topping is toasted brown and the apples are translucent and soft, 30 to 45 minutes. (Use your nose to guide you!) Check for doneness at

30 minutes. Use your Dutch oven's lid-lifter to remove the lid, being careful not to spill ash or coals into the crisp. Set the lid on a heatproof surface away from campers. (If you are not using a flanged lid, remove the hot coals with tongs and blow ash off the lid, away from people, before removing the lid.) If the crisp needs additional time, replace the lid and coals, and cook for up to 15 minutes more.

5  Serve warm directly from the Dutch oven, spooning it into each camper's bowl. (Be sure to warn your fellow campers that the pot is hot!) Drench each serving with heavy cream. Store leftovers in an airtight container, chilled, for up to 5 days.

# MOLTEN LAVA CAMPFIRE BROWNIES IN ORANGE CUPS

PREP: 30 minutes

COOK: 40 minutes

YIELD: 24 servings

---

5 ounces semisweet chocolate chips or squares

1 cup unbleached all-purpose flour

2 tablespoons unsweetened Dutch-processed cocoa powder

1 cup unsalted butter, at room temperature

1¾ cups sugar

4 eggs

1½ teaspoons vanilla extract

24 oranges

Note: These brownies are also good cooked on their own. Bake the batter in a greased 9 by 13-inch baking pan in a 350°F oven for 30 to 35 minutes, until a toothpick comes out clean. Store at room temperature for up to 4 days.

At the beginning of every season at Firelight Camps, we throw a party with our team and their families to celebrate a successful opening. I always try to make a dish over the fire, but never have I had such a throng of onlookers as the time I made orange brownie cups. The kids would have plucked them straight out of the fire if we hadn't begged them to be patient! There is something wondrous about stuffing a hollowed-out orange peel with brownie batter, baking it in a mound of coals, and then scooping out a rich, chocolate, orange-infused bite from a fruit "bowl" (which can be disposed of in the fire—the scent is glorious). Because brownie batter doesn't keep long, plan to make these your first night at camp.

---

PREP Put the chocolate chips in a heatproof bowl and set in the middle of a 12-inch sauté or frying pan. Fill the pan with 1 inch of water and bring to a simmer over medium-low heat (the bowl will begin to rattle). Turn off the heat and let the pan and chocolate sit on the burner, stirring a few times, until the chocolate is melted, 5 to 7 minutes. Let cool. (If you have a double boiler, you can use it instead to melt the chocolate.)

In a medium bowl, stir together the flour and cocoa powder with a fork.

In the bowl of a stand mixer fitted with the paddle attachment, combine the butter and sugar and beat on low speed, gradually increasing to medium, until fully incorporated and the texture is light and fluffy, about 2 minutes. Alternatively, combine the butter and sugar in a large bowl and incorporate together with your hands. Then, switch to a fork (be prepared to use some elbow grease) and beat until light and fluffy, 5 to 7 minutes.

Add the eggs, one at a time, beating well after each addition. Stir in the vanilla, followed by the melted chocolate, and mix on low speed, or with a spatula, until combined.

Fold the flour mixture into the chocolate mixture until the batter is thoroughly blended. Store in an airtight container, chilled, for up to 24 hours.

1 Prepare a campfire and let the fire burn down so that the coals are gray, ashy, and at medium heat.

2 Meanwhile, cut off the top quarter of each orange, saving the "lids." Slide a grapefruit knife or sharp paring knife between the flesh and the peel and carve around the edge so the orange flesh pulls away from the peel on all sides. Wiggle the knife under the bottom of the flesh to completely remove it from the peel, leaving behind a hollow cup. (Save the orange for adding to Campari Sangria Spritz, page 94.)

3 Fill the orange cup two-thirds of the way with brownie batter, leaving room for the brownie to expand. Replace the "lids" and wrap each orange tightly with two 10-inch sheets of heavy-duty aluminum foil.

4 Pile the coals to one side and use long tongs to place the oranges in the bottom of the campfire. Shovel coals over the oranges and let cook for 40 minutes.

5 Using the tongs, remove one orange cup and let cool enough to handle. Open the foil carefully, allowing steam to escape, and remove the "lid." You'll notice that some of the batter may have seeped out of the orange cup but the brownie should be set around the edges yet gooey in the middle, like a molten lava chocolate cake, perfect for scooping out with a spoon. If it needs more time, continue cooking for 5 to 10 minutes. Remove the remaining oranges and open the foil packets carefully to let steam escape.

6 Serve an orange directly in the foil, instructing to remove the "lid" and spoon the molten brownie straight from the cup. Store leftovers wrapped in foil, chilled, for up to 5 days.

sweet endings

# GOLDEN MILK

PREP: 2 minutes
COOK: 15 minutes
YIELD: 2 to 4 servings

---

1 teaspoon ground turmeric

½ teaspoon ground cinnamon

¼ teaspoon ground cardamom

5 turns of the pepper mill

2 cups coconut milk, almond milk, or other nondairy milk (see Note)

One 1½-inch piece fresh ginger, peeled and thinly sliced

1 teaspoon maple syrup

I once heard golden milk described as "giving the inside of your body a hug." It's sweet, spiced, and ravishingly good for you! This Ayurvedic recipe is traditionally a nightcap, a butter-yellow tonic that fortifies the immune system and aids in digestion. The fresh pepper helps release turmeric's beneficial properties. Don't heat the milk to boiling, especially with coconut milk, where the fats will rise to the top and create a slick, oily layer. If you aren't concerned about being vegan, you can use regular dairy milk and honey. This is also delicious served cold over ice.

---

**PREP** In a ziplock bag, combine the turmeric, cinnamon, cardamom, and pepper and store in a cool, dark place for up to 2 weeks.

1   In a small heavy pot over medium heat, scald the milk to just before boiling. Don't leave the milk unattended, and stir it frequently until bubbles form around the edge and the milk gives off steam, about 5 minutes. Once bubbles form, remove from the heat. Stir in the spice mixture, ginger, and maple syrup. Let steep for 10 minutes, or longer to gather more flavor.

2   Serve warm. Store leftovers in a lidded jar, chilled, for up to 3 days.

Note: If not using coconut milk, stir in ½ teaspoon coconut oil along with the maple syrup. The healthful fat makes it easier for our bodies to absorb fat-soluble turmeric.

I once awoke after an all-night bus ride through the mountains of Peru to see the regal snow-capped Cordillera de los Andes plastered against the clear, blue sky. I couldn't wait to hit the trails, but I needed to refuel and acclimatize to the thin air. My friend and I slung on our packs and beelined for a café in the town center. "It's early," said the owner, "but I have *chocolatada* on the stove." This "drinking chocolate" is typically made with melted chocolate pieces, creating a more luscious texture. My backcountry mix is made equally silky with coconut flour and arrowroot powder, and laced with the same warming spices. Add mini marshmallows for a true campfire treat, or stir the mix into your morning brew for a five-star mocha start to your day.

**PREP** In a ziplock bag, combine the cocoa powder, milk powder, cinnamon, cardamom, coconut flour, sugar, arrowroot powder, and cayenne and shake until thoroughly incorporated. Store in a cool, dark place for up to 2 weeks.

1   In a small pot or kettle, bring the water to boil.

2   In each camper's mug, combine two heaping spoons of the chocolatada mix with ¼ cup boiling water. Use the spoon to stir into a paste and top off each mug with hot water.

3   Serve immediately, topped with the marshmallow pieces.

# HOT CHOCO-LATADA

PREP: 2 minutes
COOK: 7 minutes
YIELD: 4 servings

¼ cup unsweetened Dutch-processed cocoa powder

¼ cup whole milk powder

1 teaspoon ground cinnamon

¼ teaspoon ground cardamom

2 tablespoons coconut flour

3 teaspoons granulated sugar or coconut sugar

1 teaspoon arrowroot powder

1 pinch ground cayenne, or to taste

4 cups water

2 Heavenly Vanilla Marshmallows (page 47), sliced into ¼-inch cubes

Based on the recipes in this book, I created some sample menus to help you make a meal plan. Designed like trip itineraries, the meals are listed by day. I've grouped together recipes that use the same ingredients to cut down on shopping time, storage space, and expenses. Likewise, I've accounted for how to use leftovers throughout the trip. For example, adding Grilled Eggplant and Zucchini with Zesty Za'atar (page 119) from dinner to the next evening's "Welcome to the Garden" Thai Curry (page 132). Feel free to swap out, add in, or switch around dishes. This is *your* culinary adventure!

A few tips for getting organized:

1   **Make a shopping list** based on the ingredients listed in each recipe.

2   **Make a prep list** based on the necessary Prep instructions for the recipe. Some recipes require home preparation, while others can be made completely at camp.

3   **Make an equipment list** and pack your essential outdoor kitchen (see page 12) based on the equipment called for in each method.

4   **Divide and conquer** by coordinating with fellow campers to split up shopping and prep duties and determine who's bringing what equipment.

5   **Pack your cooler** by following the recipe instructions and tips in "How to Pack Your Cooler" (page 16) for proper food storage.

# menu planners

## ADVENTURE JUNKIE

This menu is designed for a two-night trip in the backcountry, factoring in lightweight dishes that pack energy and flavor and can be cooked with minimal equipment over a backpacking stove.

TRAIL SNACKS
Maple-Rosemary Roasted
   Almond Mix (page 39)
Wild Elephant Snack Bars (page 43)
Hibiscus Lime Power-ade (page 93)
Water, water, water

### DAY 1

DINNER
Burnt Broccoli Mac 'n' Cheese
(page 152) *or* Marinara Pasta
Bake with Tuna and Capers
(page 150)

DESSERT
No-Bake Chocolate Pretzel
Power Bars (page 42)

### DAY 2

BREAKFAST
Firelight Quinoa Granola Clusters
(page 40) *with yogurt, or hard-boiled eggs with campfire toast
and* Zesty Za'atar (see page 33)

LUNCH
No-Sweat Sandwiches
(see page 76)

DINNER
Salami and Snap Pea Paella
(page 144)

DESSERT
Hot Chocolatada (page 183)

### DAY 3

BREAKFAST
Coconut-Quinoa Breakfast Bowl
with Lemon and Blueberries
(page 57; *swap fresh fruit for
dried fruit and other energy-dense
toppings like chocolate chips*)

LUNCH
No-Sweat Sandwiches
(see page 76)

menu planners

---

CAMPFIRE FOR TWO

This menu will feel like a first date at a four-star restaurant, only it's easier to make and can be enjoyed with four-star views.

TRAIL SNACKS
Ayla's Lemon–Olive Oil
    Thumbprints (page 50)
Water, water, water

**DAY 1**

HAPPY HOUR
**North Star Glühwein (page 96)** *and* **Pan con Tomate (page 105)** *with cheese and charcuterie*

DINNER
**Pan-Seared Rainbow Trout with Whole Radishes (page 155)** *and* **Lemony French Lentil Salad with Feta (page 83)**

DESSERT
*S'mores made with* **Honey Graham Crackers (page 44)** *and* **Heavenly Vanilla Marshmallows (page 47)**

**DAY 2**

BREAKFAST
**Tiramisu French Toast with Strawberries (page 72)**

LUNCH
**No-Sweat Sandwiches (see page 76)** *with* **Anytime Dill and Beet Salad (page 84)**

HAPPY HOUR
**Campari Sangria Spritz (page 94)** *and* **Maple-Rosemary Roasted Almond Mix (page 39)**

DINNER
**Crispy Lemon-Thyme Skillet Chicken with Green Beans (page 160)** *and grilled polenta* *(see page 143)*

DESSERT
**Old-Fashioned Bourbon Fool with Cherries (page 173)**

**DAY 3**

BREAKFAST
**Bird in a Nest with Honeyed Avo (page 68), British Baked Beans (page 59),** *and* **Zesty "Praline" Bacon (page 60)**

LUNCH
**Summer Squash "Pappardelle" with Basil–Sunflower Seed Pesto (page 79)** *with* **Charred Bread (page 102)** *and* **Smoked Salmon Spread (page 37)**

## DIGITAL DETOX

While a long weekend off the grid means unplugging from your gadgets, you'll be tuning in to yourself and nature more than ever before. Whether your retreat involves hiking, yoga, or meditation, this nourishing plant-based menu will help restore inner balance.

TRAIL SNACKS
**Wild Elephant Snack Bars (page 43)**
**Hibiscus Lime Power-ade (page 93)**
**Water, water, water**

### DAY 1

HAPPY HOUR
**Scorched Lemon-ade (page 92), Classic Creamy Hummus (page 34), *and* Smoky Baba Ghanoush (page 106)** *with sliced veggies*

DINNER
**Best Veggie Burger (page 136) *and* Fire-Licked Kale with Maple-Tahini Dressing (page 122)**

DESSERT
**Ayla's Lemon–Olive Oil Thumbprints (page 50)**

### DAY 2

BREAKFAST
**Firelight Quinoa Granola Clusters (page 40)** *with fresh fruit and coconut milk drizzle*

LUNCH
**Banh Mi Pad Thai Noodles (page 149)**

DINNER
**"Welcome to the Garden" Thai Curry (page 132)**

DESSERT
**Strawberry Gingersnap Chia Seed Pudding (page 172)**

### DAY 3

BREAKFAST
**Coconut-Quinoa Breakfast Bowl with Lemon and Blueberries (page 57)**

LUNCH
**No-Sweat Sandwiches (see page 76)**

## FAMILY CAMP

Soaking up the outdoors and eating together is at the core of family camping trips. On this menu, everyone will be able to find something delicious and filling to enjoy, and there's lots of opportunities for little hands to help prepare meals.

**DAY 1**

HAPPY HOUR
**Mason Jar Margs (page 97)** *and* **Camp Mess Nachos (page 110)**

DINNER
**Italian Meatball Burger (page 139)** *with* **Carol's Favorite Pasta Salad with Tomatoes, Basil, and Mozzarella (page 88)**

DESSERT
*S'mores made with* **Honey Graham Crackers (page 44)** *and* **Heavenly Vanilla Marshmallows (page 47);** *make banana boats for the kids*

**DAY 2**

BREAKFAST
**Bird in a Nest with Honeyed Avo (page 68) British Baked Beans (page 59),** *and* **Zesty "Praline" Bacon (page 60)**

LUNCH
**Classic Creamy Slaw with Pecans (page 89)** *and* **Coal-Baked Potatoes and Fixings (page 123)**

HAPPY HOUR
**Scorched Lemon-ade (page 92)** *and* **Campfire Popcorn with Sea Smoke (page 109)**

DINNER
**Zero-Degree Chili (page 147)** *and* **Dutch Oven Rosemary–Sea Salt Cornbread with Hard-Cider Butter (page 128)**

DESSERT
**Apple Harvest Crisp (page 178)**

TRAIL SNACKS
**Mamma's Famous Chocolate Chip–Banana Bread (page 49) Hibiscus Lime Power-ade (page 93) Water, water, water**

**DAY 3**

BREAKFAST
**Chocolate, Bacon, and Burrata Breakfast Sandwich (page 71)**

LUNCH
**No-Sweat Sandwiches (see page 76)**

## THE PURIST

For this menu, leave the pots and pans at home. All you need is a few utensils, a grill, and a box of heavy-duty aluminum foil.

TRAIL SNACKS

No-Bake Chocolate Pretzel
   Power Bars (page 42)
Scorched Lemon-ade (page 92)
Water, water, water

**DAY 1**

HAPPY HOUR

**Mason Jar Margs (page 97)** *and* **Camp Mess Nachos (page 110)** *with* **Guacamole in Its Shell (page 103)**

DINNER

**Fire-Licked Skirt Steak with Mamma's Salsa Verde (page 167)** *and* **Chili-Lime Festival Corn with Feta and Cilantro (page 125)**

DESSERT

**Molten Lava Campfire Brownies in Orange Cups (page 180)**

**DAY 2**

BREAKFAST

**Firelight Quinoa Granola Clusters (page 40)** *with fresh fruit and yogurt*

LUNCH

**Foil-Packet Salmon with Lemon, Thyme, and Blueberry (page 159)** *and* **Summer Squash "Pappardelle" with Basil–Sunflower Seed Pesto (page 79)**

HAPPY HOUR

*Beer or maple-laced whiskey and* **Piggies in Pajamas (page 112)**

DINNER

**Rhubarbecue Country Ribs (page 164)** *and* **Coal-Baked Potatoes and Fixings (page 123)**

DESSERT

**Grilled Stone Fruit with Bread Crumble (page 174)**

**DAY 3**

BREAKFAST

**Grilled Sausages and Polenta with Red Pepper–Fennel Kraut (page 143)** *and* **Smoky Marys with Charred Pepperoncini (page 99)**

LUNCH

**No-Sweat Sandwiches (see page 76)**

# acknowledgments

My daughter, Ayla, and the offer for *Feast by Firelight* arrived at nearly the same time, after nine months of hard work and anticipation. And for both, a village of extraordinary people was indispensable in helping me nurture each to where they are today: a toddler and a published cookbook. I feel privileged to be the one to tell this marvelous story, and I owe infinite gratitude to those who supported me, namely the team at Ten Speed Press, family and friends, recipe testers, and the Firelight Camps staff. If I forget any names on these pages, please know you are not forgotten in my heart.

The first champion of my proposal was Dennis Hayes, my book agent and an avid hiker from the Finger Lakes. Dennis introduced me to editor Veronica "Fuzzy" Randall, who, like me, was an identical twin with blonde curls and a deep reverence for the outdoors. She helped me refine this proposal and saw the offer through before losing her battle with cancer. Her spirit lives on in these pages.

The talented women at Ten Speed Press and the photography team—all avid outdoors(wo)men—have carried on that legacy. Clara Sankey, who helped me craft the final proposal; Kelly Snowden, my cunning, considerate editor and fellow outdoor junkie; Kara Plikaitis, who's clear, creative vision brought the book to life; Doug Ogan and Jane Tunks Demel for copy editing with a fine-toothed comb; Jane Chinn for overseeing production; Christina Holmes, for her transporting photography and devotion to the perfect shot; Kaitlyn Du Ross Walker, for her authentic, Herculean prop styling; Chris Lanier, for preparing fuss-free, soulful food in the field; and rock-star assistants, Spencer Wells, John Lingenfelter, and Chandley Logsdon.

To my enthusiastic recipe testers, who gave invaluable feedback. I'm indebted to Tess Le Moing, my culinary assistant, for her unflagging and exceptional work every step of the way, and to Alice Makl, Greg Tumbarello, Jason Rubenstein, Jessica Buckley, John Rowden, Jordan Bass, Kenny Lao, Kevin Buchanan, Liz Kitney, Nico Tedeyan, Rhonda Sod, and Victoria Yee.

The support from Ayla's grandparents and co-mothers was immeasurable. Olina, Ayla's "substitute mom," joined our family with exuberance, and loved and cared for our daughter as if she were her own. Thank you for giving me that rare peace of mind. Thank you to Gma Alice, Grandpa Dan, Jen Benjamin, Mamma Bear Jill, Nonna Nella, and Regina Randall for your love and reinforcement.

To my mother, Fenella Pearson, who was on-call throughout this book, and whose unconditional love and devotion are two of the greatest gifts I have ever known. I aspire to be the same kind of mother.

To Bobby, my husband, partner, best friend, and true love. *Feast by Firelight* was inspired by our business, where I was able to express my true self. Thank you for making so much daddy-daughter time so I could cook and write, and for testing and tasting countless recipes with me.

To my radiant daughter, Ayla. There is nothing more amazing than being a mother and I was aware of every moment away from you while working on this book. I hope this will be a meaningful and enjoyable gift for you one day.

To my big, incredible, international family—you're an integral part of my identity and have opened my eyes to the world. Thank you, Dimity, my identical twin and other half, for having my back *no matter what*. Your love and solidarity has allowed me to be daring and bold and you constantly inspire me. And to my siblings and best friends: Rony, Francesca, Sebastian, Lilly, Felicity, and Ophelia. Thank you, Papa, Laurence Kirwan, for encouraging me to flourish as an entrepreneur and an artist, and to my Frisch and Oppenheimer family for always believing in me.

Profound thanks to the steadfast team at Firelight Camps, who kept the fire stoked and our guests enchanted. Special appreciation for our beloved partners and ringleaders, the Wiggins Family, Greg Tumbarello, and Elaine Bobkowski—we couldn't do it without you.

To my tribe who inspired these recipes, kept me grounded, and helped me grow personally and professionally: Allison Usavage, Amber Boyd, Ana Jimenez-Kimble, Annie Brewer, Annie Farrell, Cindy Kramer, Coley Gaffney, Danielle Narveson, Dolores Siegel, Elizabeth Herendeen, Emily Gold, Emma Silverman, Ethan and Rachel Ash, Evan and Katie "MerStone" Hallas, Jessica Buckley, John Hallas, Hannah Volpi, Heather Lane, Kate Leslie, Katie Bowes,

Katie Kris, Laura Winter Falk, Leslie Bode, Lewis Freedman, Matteo Lundgren, Mark Titus, Miguel Barrios, Peaches Lyon, Pia Litz, Priscilla Timberlake, Ravi Walsh, Sara LaTorre, Sarah "Swoop" Kelsen, Shanti and Steve Mignogna, Shanshan Mei, Susan Fleming, Shoshana Perrey, and Tess Pendergrast.

I hope this book serves to honor and recognize the people, places, and natural abundance in my heart-home of the Finger Lakes. I continue to be amazed by the generosity and support of my community. Thank you to the stewards of New York State Parks for allowing us to photograph in Buttermilk Falls State Park and Taughannock State Park. The spirit of our "gorges" land is alive in this book!

Thank you to several of my favorite brands and partners who generously provided gear and food, specifically, Alaska Gold Brand, Barebones Living, Minnetonka, Narrative Space, prAna, RosieApp, The Piggery, and JAM Media Collective who provided gear from Alite Designs, BioLite, Glerups, Light & Motion, Miir, Osprey, Sunski Sunglasses, and Vuarnet France.

Finally, to Mother Earth. I hope this book encourages more people to love and care for her in the same way she cares for us.

# index

Library of Congress cataloging-in-publication Data
Names: Frisch, Emma, author.
Title: Feast by firelight : simple recipes for camping, cabins,
and the great outdoors / by Emma Frisch.
Description: First edition. | California : Ten Speed Press, [2017] |
Includes bibliographical references and index.
Identifiers: LCCN 2017030552 (print) | LCCN 2017036408
(ebook) (hardcover : alk. paper)
Subjects: LCSH: Outdoor cooking. | LCGFT: Cookbooks.
Classification: LCC TX823 (ebook) | LCC TX823 .F75 2017
(print) | DDC 641.5/78—dc23
LC record available at https://lccn.loc.gov/2017030552

Hardcover ISBN: 978-0-399-57991-2
eBook ISBN: 978-0-399-57992-9

Printed in China

Design by Kara Plikaitis

10 9 8 7 6 5 4